COMING INTO BLOOM

Coming into Bloom

Devotions through a Gardener's Eyes

BARBARA PERKINS

Tyndale House
Publishers, Inc.
Wheaton, Illinois

Scripture quotations
identified NASB are from the
*New American Standard
Bible,* copyright 1960, 1962,
1963, 1968, 1971, 1972,
1973, and 1977 by the
Lockman Foundation, and
are used by permission.

Scripture quotations
identified KJV are from the
King James Version of the
Bible.

Scripture quotations
identified TLB are from *The
Living Bible.*

Second printing, August 1988

Library of Congress Catalog Card Number
88-50023
ISBN 0-8423-0416-9
Copyright 1988 by Barbara Perkins
Printed in the United States of America

To RAYMOND, who helped it happen.

Contents

ONE
IN THE BEGINNING

And the Lord God planted a garden eastward in Eden; and there he put the man whom he had formed.

—GENESIS 2:8, KJV

TWO
WILDERNESS

My mother did not name me after Moses. Maybe she should have.

My first forty years were somewhat like his. Gentle, hopeful, well-cared-for years. I was not living in luxury in Egypt exactly, as did young Moses, but we both began life with a span of time that was relatively free of pain.

"So far, so good," I could have whispered to him across the centuries. "We're off to a good beginning, Moses."

I began a marriage, and it was a happy one. My husband and I began a life-style, a family, a scrapbook full of charming photographs of smiling faces. Life was sweet. Other families faced grief, but not ours. I began to wonder if we ever would.

In time, we did.

Our turn came to cry.

We cried over many things. It was the decade of the seventies, and many families were crying with us through the trouble of those years. So many problems in our country, in our churches, in our homes. So many pressures in our own personal lives. Family details may differ a bit, but our heartaches felt much the same.

Confusion.

Alienation.

Rejection.

Depression.

I cried out to God. He seemed not to hear. I wondered where he was in all our pain.

And then some of us lost our jobs and our financial foundations. Some of us lost our health and our emotional

10

stability. Some of us lost our dreams and our sense of purpose in life. Some of us even lost hope.

We were losers, Moses and I.

And both of us were about forty years old when we walked into a wilderness—he in Midian, I in Oklahoma.

A barren wilderness of the soul.

Crying grows tiresome in time, even in the wilderness. One longs to do something with the days besides enduring them. Moses became a keeper of the flock. I became a tiller of the ground. The two oldest occupations recorded in the family of Adam; good kinds of work to occupy thoughts and hands when Egypt or Eden is no longer home.

We'd never intended to be shepherds or gardeners, Moses and I. He'd been prepared to lead a nation and wound up leading sheep—stubborn, stupid sheep in a bleak, lonely land.

And how could I be a gardener? Why, I scarcely knew a daisy from a dandelion. And be a gardener here? The heavy clay soil around our newly acquired house was miserably hard—hard as a brick from the river-clay of Egypt.

"Were you ever discouraged, Moses? Well, so was I."

But in time—in the wilderness—we learned some lessons, Moses and I. Learned about leading flocks. Learned about growing flowers. Learned about ourselves. Learned about God.

That's what this book is all about. Lessons I learned walking a wilderness way. Disciplines and drill in a desert schoolroom. Conversations with God as I planted flowers and formed a garden in hard, red clay.

As for Moses and me, my life parallels only his learning years. But what fruitful years they became. He entered the barren wastes of Midian with only a shattered dream, yet it was there in the wilderness that Moses met God.

A loser met God?

Yes! He met God in a bush.

God in a bush? A bush in barren land?

Amazingly true!

And that's where I met him, too—except it was in a little nandina bush that I found God at work. I discovered him also in a hollyhock bed, and caught glimpses of his truths in my crop of tomatoes.

Those are the stories I want to share with you.

Do not call to mind the former things,
Or ponder things of the past.
   Behold, I will do something new,
Now it will spring forth;
Will you not be aware of it?
I will even make a roadway in the wilderness,
Rivers in the desert . . . .
   The people whom I formed for Myself,
Will declare My praise.

                    —ISAIAH 43:18-19, 21, NASB

THREE
GREEN PASTURES

Winter was fast approaching, and we needed a roof over our heads.

From the earliest days of our marriage, we had lived in other people's houses. We were a parsonage family, residing in church-owned housing, while my husband pastored churches in small towns and city suburbs. A parsonage looked good to me when it came time to move from one church to the next. I was spared the wear and tear of house hunting, and the women of the church usually had the parsonage scrubbed, painted, and apple-pie fresh by the time our moving van arrived at its door. To this day I am grateful for the kindness of those women in smoothing our transitions from city to city and church to church.

But down deep in my heart I longed for a house of our own. A house where we could paint the walls without asking permission of the House and Grounds Committee. A house that reflected our creativity and tastes. A house where I could really feel at home.

As the years went by the dream house took shape in my mind. I knew it would be built of red brick with white, wood trim—a traditional kind of house. I would hang fresh, white ruffled curtains in its windows and live there happily ever after.

Then came November, the time my husband would become the chaplain at the teaching hospital of our University of Oklahoma College of Medicine. It was time to leave the parsonage life, indeed the parsonage itself, and find a house all our own.

For weeks and weeks we had been looking at for-sale houses. We had prayed, "Lord, help us find a home." But the price tags were frightening. Where in the world would we ever find a house we could afford?

And then at dusk one day—it was a Wednesday, right after an

early evening prayer meeting at our church—we were driving through an unfamiliar section of the city. We turned a corner and saw a small, square sign lying on the ground near the curb. At dusk, down on the ground, the sign was hard to see. We pulled over to the curb, got out of our car, picked up the sign, and read it: "For Sale." Behind the fallen signpost was a big maple tree. Behind the tree was a rose-red, antique-brick house with neatly painted white, wood trim.

"This is where I want to live," said my husband.

"But the place needs a lot of work to make it like the home you see in your dreams," cautioned a realtor friend a few days later as he walked with us through the house. "Inside it's not the style and color you told me you wanted." We stared at worn wallpaper, here a wall painted black, and there one covered in a black wall-covering. "You sure you want to do it yourself? Do you two even know how?"

The repairman who came to check the heating and air-conditioning system gave us further warning: "It's a jungle of thorns around that outside compressor. I won't even consider working on it until you get all those thorn bushes out of the way." We went outside and counted the thorny pyracantha bushes that had to be trimmed—thirty-nine of them, to be exact—very mature, very tall, very tough. Not to mention a half-dozen wildly rambling rose bushes and thirty-seven other assorted shrubs.

Hedges and bushes—here, there, everywhere—all on a quarter acre of hard, red clay.

But the place certainly had possibilities. There was that towering maple tree in front, and a redbud tree as well. In the backyard there were eight flowering trees—mimosas and crab apples—and in a secluded nook a walled patio. A quiet street. Friendly neighbors. A price we could afford. A house of red brick with traditional white trim.

"We'll take it!" we decided, and eagerly signed the contract.

Moving day came shortly before Christmas. No time to decorate the usual Christmas tree, but we strung some trinkets on a juniper bush outside the patio windows and joyfully thanked the Lord for a home all our own.

"What shall we call it?" I asked, remembering the tradition of my forefathers in naming their homes, no matter how modest. There were many names of long-ago family homes I could recall.

"Island House" and "Clover Fields" and "Music Hall" and "Roundabout," all in Virginia. And as my ancestors pioneered westward they built "Sweet Canaan" and "Oak Hill" and "Springhill" and "Briarwood."

"Now what shall we call our Oklahoma home?" A house as special as this one surely needed a name.

One evening I was sitting up in bed, reading my Bible and relaxing from the hectic pace of the holidays, and I turned to the Twenty-third Psalm. "He maketh me to lie down in green pastures." "Green Pastures." What a perfect name for our home! On this lot, under this maple tree, behind these red brick walls is where the Lord has led us and now maketh us to lie down.

"Honey, know where you are?" I whispered to my husband who was snuggled under the blankets on that cold night after Christmas. "You are in 'Green Pastures.' "

"Ummm," agreed my sleepy fellow homeowner.

He maketh me to lie down in green pastures. . . . He restoreth my soul.

—PSALM 23:2-3, KJV

FOUR
THE MASTER GARDENER PROGRAM

It was the dead of winter, but inside the red brick house we felt warm and cozy. We had unloaded and thrown away the last packing box. We had repaired machineries, removed wallpaper, repainted walls, and refreshed the carpet. We had measured the windows for fresh, white ruffled curtains, and drawn up plans for future redecorating.

Green Pastures was beginning to feel like our home.

It was the dead of winter, cold and windy, but there we stood in the yard. My husband and I were ready at last to attempt to conquer the land. I was holding my father's broken-handled hoe—oh, why hadn't I taken the time to learn Dad's gardening skills while he was yet alive and tenderly growing his figs and tomatoes? And my knight in shining armor was clutching Dad's rusty saw. Together we advanced to meet "the jungle."

"Should we keep this bush? Trim off this branch? What do you think, hon?"

"I don't know. It's in the way." So we hacked and whacked and piled up three dump-truck loads of limbs and trimmings. When finally we could walk all around the house without getting assaulted by pyracantha or rose bushes or low-hanging tree limbs, we began to survey the small shrubs.

"This one looks sick. I don't know what kind of bush it is, but should any bush be khaki-colored? And this next one looks— oops, I pulled it right out of the ground. I guess you could say it looks dead."

Bush after bush, what are they? What lived alongside us here in "Green Pastures"? Did the neighbors possibly know?

"No, I don't know what you'd call those bushes. The former

16

owner, she had a real love of plants. She would know what to call them, but I sure don't know what to tell you." So said the neighbors.

Then I thought of a man at our church who knew a lot about plants. I telephoned and invited him to come give us counsel. He came over that very same day. Pencil and paper in hand, I followed him around our yard as he introduced me to plant life. Hurriedly I jotted down funny-sounding names and all sorts of tidbits of gardening information as he filled my ears with facts.

"This is Burford holly here, and Foster holly there, and this other shrub is called forsythia. That vine is wisteria, and that other vine is clematis. Over yonder is euonymus. And then there's lilac bushes and ligustrum bushes, and spirea and abelia and viburnum bushes, and further back is mock orange. My, my, you got a lot of bushes here," he said, guiding me from shrub to shrub.

And thus I consulted my friends and neighbors, family members and even garden magazines—and I was given a lot of advice, much of it conflicting. Do we prune now or in late spring? Do we plant in February or in April? Do we spray the bugs with this or that? Is there anybody here who really knows?

"Dear Lord, I'm so mixed up. I need your help. You created all this green stuff, and even the stuff that is khaki-colored now. Please, Lord, help me figure out what to do with it."

I enrolled in a class for beginning gardeners at our local community college. And it was there I found an answer to my needs: The Master Gardener program. I learned I could call the Oklahoma State University Extension Center and speak directly to a master gardener to get true, personalized answers to all my questions.

I rushed to the telephone. "Hello, is this the master gardener? . . . Whew, am I glad to find you!"

And later on, speaking to God, I said,

"Lord, things are looking brighter now in 'Green Pastures.' I am getting some help and learning to make sense of this yard work. Who knows, what started out as self-defense hedge-trimming might yet turn out to be fun! Maybe I'll even get a new hobby out of this. Imagine that! Me, a gardener!

"But surprisingly, Lord, I see plants in a different light now. It's as though your garden parables are coming to life before my eyes. And strange to say, I am beginning to see you from a different perspective, too.

"Today, for instance, as I was talking to that local master gardener, I thought of you, Lord. That's a good name for you! You are the ultimate, divine Master Gardener, far and high above passing opinions and conflicting counsel here on earth. I've never thought of you that way before or known that part of your personhood.

"Truly, you are the great I AM, the personal name you revealed to Moses. I AM the way, the truth, the life. I AM the good shepherd. I AM the resurrection. I AM the living water, the bread of life, the light of the world. I AM the alpha and the omega, the first and the last, the beginning and the end. I AM the answer.

"I AM—forever, in Moses' generation as well as in mine.

"I AM—forever, whatever our needs.

"Thank you, Lord—Master Gardener—Sir.

"I am grateful."

To whom then will you liken God? . . .
It is He who sits above the vault of the earth . . .
Who stretches out the heavens like a curtain. . . .
    "To whom then will you liken Me
That I should be his equal?" says the Holy One.

The grass withers, the flower fades, but the Word of our God stands forever.

—ISAIAH 40:18, 22, 25, 8, NASB

FIVE
DESIGN AND DEVELOPMENT

"A homeowner should have a five-year plan for landscape design and development," said the teacher of my gardening class. I took notes as fast as I could, not wanting to miss a single word of his wisdom.

"Not many people can afford the time or the money to redesign a landscape all at once," he continued.

"Amen," I murmured to myself, thinking of our limited budget and all too few opportunities to spend much time making over a yard. My husband's work as a chaplain required overtime and even some weekend hours, and my job as a secretary was keeping me plenty busy. Still we had a longing for pretty things, some green grass, some healthy bushes, maybe even some flowers.

My mind returned to class. The teacher was making an assignment: "Take into consideration your house style, your available time for yard work now and yard maintenance later, how long you plan to live there, plus any possibilities for future improvements on your grounds. Then draw for me your ideal plan to scale on graph paper. Will your design be formal or informal? Symmetrical or asymmetrical?"

Beats me, I thought wearily. *This is getting complicated.*

The teacher lectured on and on. "However formal or informal your landscape plan, you will need certain elements within that design, such as simplicity of statement, balance of lines, rhythm and flow, proportion, and color, and a contrast of textures. Above all else you must have a focal point. Now what will be your center of focus for each view of your yard?"

What indeed! my mind responded in panic. *I came here to learn how to plant something pretty in the bare spots, and how to keep the hedges from swallowing us whole. And now you tell me I* must know what we'll want five years in advance, and draw that design to scale on graph paper—and besides that, have a center of focus for each view? Whew!

I was tempted to give up. To "throw in the trowel" on gardening. Was it worth the effort?

And God said,

They that sow in tears shall reap in joy. He that goeth forth and weepeth, bearing precious seed, shall doubtless come again with rejoicing, bearing his sheaves with him.

—PSALM 126:5-6, KJV

SIX
WINTER DAY

I sat beside the window, looking out at winter. It was February inside and out. I felt old and cold, weighed down with the unresolved problems and still-raw pains of the past ten years. I sat wrapped up in sorrow, a sorrow like an old gray sweater that is unattractive but comfortably familiar on a cold day in winter.

Outside I saw the maple tree, bare and blown by the wind. It looked twisted and blackened and frazzled. A perfect picture of my February self.

There was an empty flower bed just below the window. I glanced at the crusted seedbed and for the first time really studied it. Hard clay dirt, trampled down and badly cracked. How could anything grow in such hard dry ground? What miracle would it take to make that soil soft, fertile, productive, brimming with life and color?

That day I had no answer.

"God, where are you in this bitter coldness? I am shriveled, frozen, barren—as barren as that maple tree twisting in the wind. My soul feels as dry and cracked as that ugly, empty flower bed.

"Where have you been these ten long years?

"I prayed.

"You seemed silent.

"Things went from bad to worse.

"You let them.

"In Psalm 95 I read, 'Today if ye will hear his voice, harden not your heart,' but today I do not hear or feel anything of you.

"Where are you, God?

"Can spring come again to the crusted ground? to the twisted tree? and to me?"

Dear Lord, if indeed I am Thine,
If Thou art my sun and my song,
Say, why do I languish and pine,
And why are my winters so long?

Oh, drive these dark clouds from my sky;
Thy soul-cheering presence restore;
Or take me unto Thee on high,
Where winter and clouds are no more.

—"How Tedious and Tasteless"
JOHN NEWTON (1725–1807)

SEVEN
UNDER OBSERVATION

"What is this little bush way back here in the corner?" I asked a neighbor one late winter morning as we paused from our chores to chat a bit across the fence. "It is small but greening now, and struggling to survive. What is it?"

My neighbor didn't know, and when I asked my relatives and friends, neither did they. If it were a weed bush, shouldn't I then get rid of it? But what if it were a good bush? What was it?

The Unknown Bush, that's what it was.

Over a period of time I began to take a liking to that little bush. Maybe its being unnamed and unknown aroused my curiosity. At any rate I one day gently dug it up from its cramped, sunless site and replanted it in a spacious, sunny, well-watered location. With some cultivation and some tender care, perhaps it would reveal itself to me.

You know what? The Unknown Bush blossomed yellow all over! A most dazzling sight after the blacks and whites of winter. And later on some small, green berries began to form, berries that eventually turned a shiny dark purple. I consulted my new gardening book.

"Why, this plant appears to be a currant bush. A golden-flowering *Ribes aureum*, it says here. Distinctive green leaves. Yellow flowers. Purple fruit. Just like ours!

"Now I know you, little bush. You yourself told me what you are."

And I said to God, "We give away our secret selves by our blooms and our berries, don't we?"

And he said,

You will know them by their fruits.

—MATTHEW 7:16, NASB

23

EIGHT
THE PAIN OF PRUNING

Now what should we do with the mock orange bush?

Planted years ago in a too-crowded spot, butchered last January when we hacked off its branches, its appearance was a mockery, for sure. A mockery of its true beauty pictured in my new gardening book. It should have fragrant white flowers and long, curving branches, but it didn't. Not any more!

But what if . . . ? What if we dug it up and moved it to a wide open space? So what if, in being transplanted, it would then need to be cut back again? For the first time in years our mock orange could start life over—begin anew—and become the pretty plant the Master Gardener designed it to be.

So we dug it up, my husband and I. If bushes feel pain, surely this one was in agony as we attempted to improve its lot in life. We lost a great deal of the root system in the digging process, for its roots went way under the house. And then we had to compensate for all that loss by cutting back its top branches. So, from a former height of six misshapen feet, after our uprooting and pruning the mock orange bush ended up about nine inches tall.

To have seen us wrestling with the roots and whacking at the limbs, one might think we despised that plant, or took some sort of sadistic pleasure in abusing helpless bushes.

But that perception would have been wrong, false. In truth we liked that battered bush. We wanted to see it become shapely, showy, in full-blown maturity. So we strained our backs, dirtied our hands, struggled—all because of concern, not contempt.

Was it worth the pain of pruning?

Well, if bushes had beauty pageants, our mock orange could now be a winner!

"Lord, see what we did to the mock orange bush? We really

worked it over, didn't we? But I learned something today as I worked on my bush. I learned about cutting loose, and I learned about moving on.

"I want to remember this day and my dealings with that bush the next time I sense you're dealing with me; cutting away old habits and entanglements that tie me down; pruning off misshapen parts of personality and character; moving me from the old and familiar to the new and unknown.

"It hurts. Oh, it hurts! I tend to take the hurt I feel as a sure sign of your rejection, your punishment, or your abuse of me.

"But now, Lord, help me to see my prunings through wiser eyes, as I reshaped this bush—and you reshape me."

I know, O Lord, that Thy judgments are righteous,
And that in faithfulness Thou hast afflicted me.
—PSALM 119:75, NASB

NINE
A WORLDWIDE VIEW

When I began to observe plants, I was fascinated by their endless variety. There surely were a lot of green things to choose from in designing a five-year garden plan.

The time period mentioned in the first chapter of Genesis, when God created plant life, must have been a day of joyful imagination and celebration. Oh, the dramatic and infinite variety of colors and shapes and textures and fragrances he created. I wished I could grow some of everything he made in my garden.

The redbud tree in our front yard, I knew, was the state tree of Oklahoma. The state flower—the mistletoe—was also growing in our neighborhood. But what of the other ornamentals and garden plants I admire? Were they Oklahoman or what?

I did some reading in my gardening book and found that most of my favorites came here from faraway shores.

For example, chrysanthemums and peonies came from eastern Asia. Wisteria came from Japan to this continent courtesy of a physician who traveled around the world. Asia was also the original home of day lilies and Easter lilies, forsythia and holly and ligustrum bushes, as well as crab apple trees—all growing now in "Green Pastures."

India or Burma was once home to our crape myrtle bushes, while the lilacs and pyracantha hedge came from Mediterranean countries. Someday I would add tulips and poppies to our garden, and they too would come from the Mediterranean coast.

The following summer I would plant petunias and cannas and caladiums—all from South America. From Mexico would come our marigolds for summer enjoyment, and then poinsettias for Christmas cheer.

The ivy, and the iris bed? And later on some pansies? They once grew together in the southern part of Europe.

And as for hanging baskets of geraniums and begonias and asparagus fern, all of these beauties came from Africa.

I was excited, for all of these are citizens of the world, to be coming together and finding fellowship around our home—a blooming United Nations. Each in its own way had much to offer. I would be foolish indeed to limit my design and my Oklahoma garden to just a redbud tree and a mass of mistletoe—just our kind of plants.

"Creator, Lord, how you must enjoy your ingenious inventions. You could have stopped when you designed one kind of flower, but instead you filled the world with variety. Exciting, mind-boggling variety.

"A variety of people, too. You created so many kinds and colors and shapes and sizes. No two exactly alike. A dizzying diversity.

"Teach me to be open-hearted—as you are, Lord—to more than just mistletoe and redbud trees and 'our kind' of companions."

TEN
SUPPORT GROUPS

This new hobby of gardening was a lift to my spirits, a challenge to my skills. As I drove through the park on my way to work, or ran my errands on residential streets, or took a trip through the countryside, I grew increasingly interested in plant life.

I studied the wild, natural settings to see how trees and bushes and flowers grew there. And then in well-designed city landscapes, I again analyzed the arrangements of plants. I watched for ways to use plant materials to best advantage in color and impact.

So often the best advantage, in both wild and well-manicured sites, was to create a grouping of plants. A cluster of three or five or more.

A shady green grove of pine trees.

A roadside border of orange sumac.

A massed bed of red-hot salvia.

A group makes a stronger visual statement than one tree or bush or bedding plant alone. Just picture one little pansy huddled by itself in a flower border. How lost it would look. How much more beautiful for pansies to be a thick, colorful carpet of blooms than just isolated individuals.

"Lord of hosts, how consistent you are in that you created all of us earthlings to find strength in community. How we need each other! No wonder you gave us groups—the forest, the flock, the herd, the hive, the family, the church. The group of many who support the one."

God setteth the solitary in families.

—PSALM 68:6, KJV

Let us consider how to stimulate one another to love and good deeds, not forsaking our own assembling together, as is the habit of some, but encouraging one another. . . .

—HEBREWS 10:24-25, NASB

ELEVEN
DAY BEFORE EASTER

It was the Saturday before Easter—and I was waiting. Waiting for some sign of life in a ligustrum bush.

We'd had a harsh, cold December, much colder and drier than usual. Even so, most of our bushes were sprouting new leaves. All except one—the ligustrum.

Was it dormant? Dead?

I waited for one leaf to give me hope for life still within.

The Saturday before Easter. A waiting day.

And has it not been a waiting day for two thousand years?

My thoughts went back in time to that first day before Easter when in stunned inactivity, frozen with fear, the friends of Jesus waited. And wondered. And hoped. And doubted. And watched for morning to come.

In their anxiety, did they remember the words of the psalmist? How often during these past ten years have those words come to my mind:

I wait for the Lord, my soul does wait.
And in His word do I hope.
My soul waits for the Lord
More than the watchmen for the morning;
Indeed, more than the watchmen for the morning.
—PSALM 130:5-6, NASB

I looked once again at the leafless bush. "Are you still you, ligustrum? The ligustrum that once was alive? I have fine plans for you. If you don't fill your place in the garden, there will be such a gap. I wait and I watch you for some sign of life."

And then I turned to God:

"The Saturday before Easter—and I wonder, Lord, if you are

30

not also waiting and watching. Waiting, and watching me for some sign of life.

"Am I dormant? Dead?

"Such a cold winter of the soul these ten years—and did my inner self wither away in the unusually harsh storms of life? Are you waiting for me to warm and stir and become what you planned in the beginning—and maybe even yet bloom?

"Help us, Lord of Easter mornings. We need you, the ligustrum and I."

TWELVE
TRANSPLANTING

"I think we've dug up and transplanted every bloomin' thing in our yard at least three times," I heard my husband remark to a friend.

I think he was half-complaining and half-bragging about his labor. And labor it truly was. He had every right to feel those sore arm muscles and that pride of accomplishment—along with bewilderment at my sudden urges to rearrange the yard "furniture."

There was that scrawny nandina bush I discovered barely surviving, below and behind a tall holly hedge. It was growing in the dark, jammed behind the holly and the house. I took mercy on the poor thing and moved it from those cramped quarters to a wider, sunnier place beside the patio.

But somehow as my patio plan evolved from one design to another, the nandina no longer fit in with its surroundings. So I moved it again to a spot near the fence.

However, it did not thrive there. Too much heat and too little moisture perhaps. The only decent thing to do, at least as I saw it, was to move the nandina yet again.

And now at this writing, it is planted and prospering in the front yard near the entrance to our home. Here there's a balance of sun and moisture, plus protection from wind, and room to grow.

"Blessings on you, little bush. I think I've finally planted you in just the right place."

And then I said to God: "My husband is perplexed, Lord, at all my transplanting. And the nandina? No telling what it feels about its recent uprootings. But just look at it grow now. Look at it flourish. Lots of leaves, blooms, and berries. Look how I helped it! Transplanting—it's the caring thing to do.

"And Lord, what I do to my plants, I think you do to me. Time and again you've found me stuck in some unhealthy circumstance—and you've lifted me up and moved me to a wider space. A growing place with a fresh, new view.

"Sometimes I didn't want to move. Or change. Or do anything but sit there.

"You moved me, anyhow. You are a transplanter, too, I see.

"And now here we are in 'Green Pastures,' transplanting and being transplanted. I have good plans for that nandina, and you, Lord, have plans for me. Good plans, I think—plans worth my pain. So I will trust myself to your hands as you move me from where I am to where I ought to be. You promised, 'I am with you alway, even unto the end of the world.' And if that's where I wind up living—at the end of the world—knowing you are with me in the moves is all I really need to know."

THIRTEEN
A PARABLE OF TOMATOES

The parables of Jesus were not new to me. As a child I had
learned of his teachings. I had trusted him as my Savior when I
was fourteen years old. I had read the Bible through again and
again. But now it seemed as though I were hearing his truths for
the very first time, particularly his parables.

Sheep-keeping.

Seed-sowing.

Jesus, creator of sheep, designer of flowers, told such simple
stories of herding and gardening. I had studied them in college,
taught them in Sunday school. But I'd never really absorbed
them—not as now, from a gardener's point of view.

Consider this story:

*And He said, "To you it has been granted to know the mysteries
of the kingdom of God, but to the rest it is in parables. . . .*

"Now the parable is this: the seed is the word of God.

*"And those [seed] beside the road are those who have heard;
then the devil comes and takes away the word from their heart, so
that they may not believe and be saved.*

*"And those [seed] on the rocky soil are those who, when they
hear, receive the word with joy; and these have no firm root; they
believe for a while, and in time of temptation fall away.*

*"And the seed which fell among the thorns, these are the ones
who have heard, and as they go on their way they are choked with
worries and riches and pleasures of this life, and bring no fruit to
maturity.*

*"And the seed in the good soil, these are the ones who have
heard the word in an honest and good heart, and hold it fast, and
bear fruit with perseverance."*

—LUKE 8:10-15, NASB

34

Let me tell you about the tomato plants in the backyard.

We set them out in April, and I remember how hard we worked to prepare the ground. We had to break up the soil and dig out the rocks. We had to pour in powdered gypsum to soften the clay. We had to fertilize regularly, water weekly, and shelter the soil with a cottonseed mulch. All in high hopes of a coming harvest.

Was the effort worthwhile?

Well, if you'd seen those tall tomato plants spangled with red-ripe fruit from July to September, you'd know our hard work was richly rewarded.

"Lord, look at those tomatoes!

"We perspired. You blessed. Together we made a good crop.

"But in moments of quietness, when I read your Word and examine my life, I see there is yet harder work to do than preparing our ground for tomatoes. Now I must deal with me.

"Not only in the garden but also in my heart, I find the success of tomorrow lies in the seedbed of today.

"Lord, help me prepare this seedbed within. Soften the hardness. Root out the weeds. Harvest time is coming, and you'll be looking for a crop.

"If only my fruit-bearing could keep pace with those tomato plants!"

FOURTEEN
DENOMINATIONAL DIFFERENCES

In April I designed a patriotic flower border around the patio. I envisioned red geraniums rising up from a paving of white alyssums, flanked by blue ageratums and backed by blue veronicas. To my eyes those red, white, and blue colors blend beautifully in a garden—contrasting, complementing, creating a balanced look. Carefully I patted each bedding plant into place, hoping for harmony of color come summer and the Fourth of July.

May arrived, and my flowers were looking good together. I watered and weeded and impatiently waited for the coming burst of brilliance.

By the first of June each plant had tripled in size and had come into bloom. The alyssums became a lush carpet of low-lying, snow-white blossoms, from which red geraniums rose in all their crimson splendor. Behind them waved the vivid spikes of massed blue veronicas. And filling in the in-between spaces, the matching blue ageratums completed the pleasing picture. Together they looked like Old Glory fluttering in the wind.

"Good for you, guys," I praised the plants. "You're doing fine, beautifying and framing the patio. How well you work together! What an inspiring sight to see!"

But then in mid-June we had heavy rains followed by a sizzling summery heat wave. I guess the alyssums didn't like wet feet. Some gave up and quit blooming. Others turned pale, and pouted, and seemed to withdraw from the garden fellowship.

The geraniums, however, liked the water—and indeed demanded more. The blue veronicas and ageratums tried to be agreeable, staying neutral in the dispute, but feelings were clearly rising in the garden community.

I waited a week or ten days before watering, in deference to the ailing alyssums. But by then the red-hot geraniums were in an ugly mood. "Give us water, or we'll wilt on you!" They meant it, too.

So I gave the garden a watering, whereupon the alyssums just gave up for good. "Too much water!" they wailed as they withered and died.

"Bring on the water!" roared the red-faced geraniums, uncaring and unsympathetic to the roots.

"Hey, can't we work out some way to live here together?" pleaded the peace committee of veronicas and ageratums. "Why all this uproar over water?"

By the Fourth of July—when all my expectations had pointed to a flower bed of special significance, even grandeur—all I had left was an eyesore. Just some overexpanded, arrogant geraniums lording it over some intimidated ageratums and leaning hard on some valiant veronicas. The border had become a battlefield littered with dead heaps of alyssums, no longer white now but a deathbed brown. Evidently they would rather not be at all than to work out water arrangements with their red and blue buddies.

Ruined by discord, the community of plants was a disaster area. Not at all the design I'd intended.

"Aw shucks, fellas," I sighed as I carted off alyssum corpses and replanted the border. "Why couldn't you learn to live together in peace?"

And I think the Master Gardener who designed and then made us all was saddened as well. He understood my disappointment. He, too, had once planned and planted a garden.

Behold, how good and how pleasant it is
For brothers to dwell together in unity!

—PSALM 133:1, NASB

FIFTEEN
YOU REAP WHAT YOU SOW

Take it from one who knows, the first year a person attempts to grow a garden is going to be a year of guesswork and "Guess what?"

I think each novice gardener should be issued a beginner's permit and not be allowed inside a garden center if not chaperoned by an agent of the U.S. Department of Agriculture.

I was like a baby let loose in a candy store that first year each time I went to a garden center. Everything on the premises looked to me both tempting and terrifying. Should I buy that beauty? Could it survive my care? The colorful pictures on the plant tags were enticing, yet the formidable and funny names made me wonder if anything that exotic could possibly feel at home in Oklahoma. My feet would be aching, not to mention my head, before I finally made choices and departed with my purchases.

That's how I ended up with some *gypsophila paniculata*, a *dicentra spectabilis*, three delphiniums and two *gaillardia aristatas*, along with a little lupine and a handful of hostas. (Don't those names just give you goose bumps?)

Though I had them in my possession, I didn't know much about them. But they looked pretty, and they were bargain-priced, and it just felt good to have been at the garden center, as though I were a real live gardener.

I planted all those beguiling plants in the wrong places. I didn't mean to, but I did anyhow. And when they started growing, they weren't at all what I had anticipated.

For instance, the delphiniums could not hold up their heads in our Oklahoma winds, so they looked stooped and stupid all their brief lives in my garden.

And as for the gaillardias, they turned out much broader than pictured, and certainly didn't fit in the space I'd allowed for them.

The lupine was sulky all season, the dicentra turned from green to gray, and the hostas never made it up past ground-level.

All in all, I got what I paid for, but I also got what I really did not want. And two months after a purchase, it is hard to return straggly bedding plants to the garden center and ask for your money back.

God said,

Be not deceived . . . whatsoever a man soweth, that shall he also reap.

—GALATIANS 6:7, KJV

"Lord, I know. I know NOW.

"Like Hosea and Solomon said, you sow the wind, and you reap the whirlwind. You sow iniquity; you reap vanity.

"But I didn't think they were talking to me.

"I thought I could sow some bargains and reap *Better Homes and Gardens*."

SIXTEEN
A HINT OF MINT

The days were getting longer and sunnier. An Oklahoma summer was headed our way, frying-pan hot.

And what is summer without a frosty glass of iced tea? And what is summer tea without a fresh mint leaf floating in the glass?

That's why, when I saw a wasted little mint plant in the potting shed of the garden center, alone on the back shelf, wilted and ready to die, I had to bring it home with me. Such a tiny, innocent herb. Such potential to spice up my summertime tastes. I planted it in my flower border and began to anticipate the iced-tea days ahead.

The mint plant did very well indeed. Soon there were enough leaves for tea for the whole neighborhood. And when the mint plant bloomed, it attracted a pastel-pretty cloud of butterflies hovering over its blossoms. What a delightful plant, this mint!

But as days turned into months, and months became seasons, the mint plant lost its innocence. It grew so thick and bulky it filled up one flower border, and then it popped up alarmingly in the two adjoining beds. Mint leaves began to emerge in the Bermuda grass beside the beds, crowding out everything in their path. When my husband ran the lawnmower over that area, there was a refreshing scent of mint—but what a high price to pay for air freshener! Now our recently-reseeded lawn was fighting for its life against the onward-marching mint. In time we came to call it the Enemy.

Eventually it was the Enemy or us. Either we would get rid of the mint, or the mint would take over our yard. The battle was on—and oh, how we underestimated the Enemy.

First, my husband and I tried to trim it down to size. When trimming did not control the mint, we tried to hoe it out. When hoeing proved hopeless, we tried to dig it out. Then we had to go back again and dig still deeper, and dig deep over a long period of time, and exercise weekly watchfulness, and sometimes even resort to high-powered poison to kill out the stubborn stuff.

It took a long time, and gritty fingernails and gritted teeth, but we finally won our war with the Enemy. And to think it all started with such a tiny sprout.

"Just a hint of mint, Lord. That's all it was. A teeny taste.

"Your Apostle Paul might have been a food hobbyist, for he wrote in Galatians 5, 'A little leaven leavens the whole lump.'

"But had he been a gardener like me, I think he would have written, 'Give mint an inch, and it will take a yard.' "

SEVENTEEN
A TIME TO PLANT AND A TIME TO PLUCK

That spring I planted a small patch of sweet william under the wisteria arbor that shelters the garden gate. Dear sweet william—fresh, fragrant, old-fashioned. I enjoyed the upturned faces of my rosy Wee Willie day by day as I passed back and forth under the arch.

But then July came and with it blistering heat. The overwhelming simmer of an Oklahoma summer. I withdrew from the outdoor broiler, retreating indoors to make icy lemonades and walk barefoot on the cool kitchen floor, closing the curtains to keep out the blazing glare of seething sunshine.

One evening after the fierce heat of the day subsided, I went outdoors to see the sweet william patch. The sight caught me by surprise. Gone were the blooms, and shriveled were the leaves. A few seed pods—and that was all. No more rosy faces. No more Wee Willies.

I really had not planned to say good-bye so soon.

"Lord, look what a mess! I didn't remember to water them. I was so busy keeping cool myself that I forgot the Wee Willies were out here roasting in the heat wave. Look how withered they are!"

I thought of the Ninetieth Psalm—and of Moses, grown old and probably feeling withered himself the day he wrote its words. We are like grass, he said—or like a patch of sweet william.

In the morning it flourishes, and sprouts anew;
Toward evening it fades, and withers away. . . .
So teach us to number our days,
That we may present to Thee a heart of wisdom.
—PSALM 90:6, 12, NASB

And I said to God, "Growing season truly is a limited number of days, isn't it, Lord? I did not realize how soon the bloom would fade. Such a lovely beginning. Such a beautiful spring. Day after day, taken for granted. But then spring turned to summer, gentle rain gave way to searing wind—and then came the blasting heat.

"That's life, I suppose. The seasons change—and there's a limit to growing and blooming and scattering seed.

"And those haunting words of Moses—they remind me that my time, too, is limited. A limited time to come into bloom. A limited time to grow as a person, to mature as a Christian, to develop a heart of wisdom. A limited time to prepare for you a harvest. A limited time to scatter some seed that may later come forth in next-generation Christians.

"I guess I'd presumed springtime would never end."

I plucked up the browned, brittle plants. "Good-bye, sweet william. Did you reproduce your beauty in next season's seed? I hope you've done your work well. There was so little time, you know."

And God said,

To every thing there is a season . . . A time to be born, and a time to die; a time to plant, and a time to pluck up that which is planted.

—ECCLESIASTES 3:1-2, KJV

EIGHTEEN
THE CUTTING EDGE OF COMPASSION

Each day now there was something to be watered. I dragged our garden hoses in never-ending circles around and around our house. Back and forth went the oscillating sprinklers, drenching everything in their paths. I thought I was doing my world a favor.

"Better watch out for hollyhock rust," warned a more experienced gardener. "It can become a serious problem here with hollyhocks. It's pretty obvious when plants are infected with it because yellow or orange spots with red centers appear on the topsides of their leaves. Overhead watering that way," he glanced at the sprinkler spray, "can make it worse."

I hurried over to my lovely cluster of hollyhocks, higher than my head and blazoned with blooms. I looked closely at their leaves. What do you know! They had rusted.

"Once rust attacks a plant," continued my friend, "it enters the tissues. Only way to fight it is to cut off the infected leaves. You may have to cut off a right smart number of leaves—maybe even stalks, too—or you'll wind up losing your plants altogether."

But to cut off the leaves and stems of my prized hollyhocks? Surely there was an easier remedy for rust than that.

So I held back on overhead watering and instead soaked only the roots with a slow-running hose. I bought a jar of fungicide and sprayed the plants weekly to kill out the fungus. I even yanked off a few of the worst-looking leaves.

Did this help?

Not a bit.

Finally I had to do the unthinkable: cut a lot of hollyhocks to the ground in order to save the rest of the plants.

On my knees in the dirt, butcher knife in hand and eyeball-to-eyeball with hollyhock rust, I learned some things that day about contamination. And there in the dirt, cutting down hollyhocks, some Old Testament stories of Moses and the Israelites took on new meaning for me.

It was Moses who warned his people about the polluting influence of pagan gods, especially the idolatry of Baal worship:

Now, therefore hearken, O Israel. . . . Your eyes have seen what the Lord did because of Baal-peor: for all the men that followed Baal-peor, the Lord thy God hath destroyed them from among you. But ye that did cleave unto the Lord your God are alive every one of you this day.

—DEUTERONOMY 4:1, 3-4, KJV

Again Moses commanded his people,

When the Lord thy God shall bring thee into the land whither thou goest to possess it, and hath cast out many nations before thee . . . thou shalt smite them, and utterly destroy them; thou shalt make no covenant with them, nor shew mercy unto them. . . . Thine eye shall have no pity upon them: neither shalt thou serve their gods; for that will be a snare unto thee.

—DEUTERONOMY 7:1-2, 16, KJV

"Lord, it seemed a cruel and heartless step to take—cutting my hollyhocks down to the ground. But if that's what it takes to remove the snare, to stop the dying and save the living, I guess it's the only loving thing to do.

"That was your decision, too, I recall."

NINETEEN

THE ONE AMONG THE MANY

If once we found a plant we really liked, my husband and I had a tendency to march right over to the garden center and buy a bunch of them. I mean, a *bunch*.

Can you believe we bought twenty-eight more holly bushes?

I was attempting, according to the gardening book, to create a sense of unity in design by repeating a common element. In this case, holly. But too much of anything can become monotonous. Too much of anything, and the yard looks overrun with "weeds." Even holly weeds. That's how I began to appreciate the value of the individual.

The one among the many.

The individual is a surprise, a needed element in a landscape plan. A purple-leafed flowering plum tree inlaid like a jewel in a mostly green setting—now there's a nice surprise for the eyes. On a smaller scale, one clump of white petunias framed by fiery red salvia—now there's a bold break in monotony.

As time passed I began to value the individual, the one specimen plant, more and more. One of my favorite individuals was a large pyracantha bush we trimmed into tree form. We cut away all lower branches, exposing its gnarled inner framework, but the top branches were left to become a fifteen-foot-tall umbrella. This rustic, twisted, multi-trunked tree bore white flowers in spring, orange berries in fall, and green leaves year-round. It became the focal point—the exclamation point—of our patio garden.

Another favorite individual was the tropical candle tree that grew in one summer from a mere twig of ten inches to a giant, as tall as my husband and eight feet wider.

An interesting unique characteristic of this candle tree was its habit of folding up its foliage at sunset. Like an enormous prayer plant that my mother used to have—or like a "spiritual giant" as one of our sons called it—the candle tree folded its leaves as though they were hands in prayer. From sundown until sunup the tree maintained a "praying" appearance. And in the fall, when most other plants were calling it quits for the season, the candle tree was all aflame with bright yellow candlelike blooms. A real standout in a crowd, this candle tree.

And I said to God, "I praise your wisdom in not creating us all alike. Yet sometimes, Lord, I've thought that being alike was the answer to perfect unity. Unity in a marriage. Unity in a family. Unity in a church. If we were alike, wouldn't we understand each other better, work together more productively, live together more predictably?

"But now I'm beginning to see—with you—the worthiness of the individual, and the welcome relief the one brings to the many. The rare statesman, the uncommon inventor, the prodigy at the piano, the offbeat personality who brightens a party—the one, a little bit different from the group and very special.

"Help me, Lord, to appreciate those who surprise me—in landscapes and in life."

TWENTY
TEAMWORK

Our first summer in "Green Pastures" was coming to a close. The last of August was here, bringing with it thoughts of a Labor Day cookout. A fitting end to a full summer in which both my garden and my very soul had been under cultivation.

Lemonade glass in hand, I went out to sit on the patio and plan a Labor Day menu. I chose a shaded spot on the steps for my sitting and thinking place. "Hamburgers. Potato salad. Baked beans. Banana pudding . . ."

I stretched out my legs, relaxed my shoulders. The heat of the afternoon drained away the muscle tension and left me quietly, contentedly limp.

Sitting there on the patio, surveying the garden scene, I let my thoughts ramble back to long-ago memories. Memories of years when I dreamed of having our very own house. A red-brick-with-white-trim house. Come to think of it, that dream house always did have a garden setting. Shade trees and rose bushes and flowers by the door. I knew very little about plant life then, but even to an amateur dreamer a garden seemed a necessary ingredient in a dream about dream-houses.

Ingredient.

"Oh yes, ingredients," I murmured. My mind returned to the task at hand. "I'll need bananas, vanilla wafers, some sweetened condensed milk. . . ."

But it was hard to think of a grocery list when the beauty of the garden kept claiming my attention. The patio border seemed aglow that afternoon: sunny-yellow marigolds, rosy-red impatiens, blue ageratums, and matching blue veronicas. Garden ingredients I'd brought to our home.

How long we'd waited to call a house "our home."

48

And as the years had gone by how often I wondered if this house of my dreams had yet been built, and if the current owners were planting a garden around it. What would they choose for their flower borders? I wondered if we would ever find the place—and if we found it, would we like what they'd planted? Somehow I had sensed it was more than an idle daydream, this home to come. The thought of it—the anticipation—would set my heart racing.

Now, years later, the dream had come true. I lazily leaned my back against the reality of red brick walls warmed by the sun. And yes, those former owners did plant likable things around our home. I could look about me here, there, yonder, all around "Green Pastures," and see how their work had endured. Garden ingredients, still fresh and productive.

A surge of thanksgiving welled up within me and crowded out my menu planning. I was grateful for the maple tree somebody planted so we could rest in its shade, and the grandchildren could play croquet in summer and still feel cool beneath its canopy.

And here on the patio I celebrated the shelter of the vines, the fragrant arbor of honeysuckle and sweet autumn clematis that turned the patio into a perfumed bower when they bloomed. Planted by someone else's hands, they still breathed a blessing on our May and August evenings.

I looked toward the flower borders beyond, and let my thoughts run away to a distant past. Somebody at some time collected a dozen kinds of irises and planted them here on this plot of ground. And years before that, somebody brought irises to Oklahoma, probably in a covered wagon. To her it must have been a touch of home she brought to this raw, new land. How crowded her wagon must have been, full to overflowing with children and quilts and furniture and tools. And yet she found room to squeeze in a few brown rhizomes of irises. A bit of yesterday to take to tomorrow. I am indebted to that unknown iris-lover, that pioneer woman who gifted the previous homeowners with irises, who in turn gifted me.

Today—this happy day at the end of August—I am both reaping and sowing. Enjoying the benefits of things planted before me, and taking my turn to till the soil now—planting still more for those who come after me.

I lifted my glass of lemonade as a toast. "Future homeowner, I salute you! I salute you with poppies and daisies and big blue liriope you're going to love."

Sowing and reaping, we rejoice together in separate centuries. And God said,

What joys await the sower and the reaper, both together! For it is true that one sows and someone else reaps. I sent you to reap where you didn't sow; others did the work, and you received the harvest.

—JOHN 4:36-38, TLB

TWENTY-ONE
WHEN THE WEEDS ARE WINNING

As an amateur gardener, I fought a never-ending, often-losing war with weeds.

Weeds rose up all around us. Weeds on parade in all shapes and sizes. Weeds on the march in all battlefield conditions. I fought them wherever I found them, and sometimes I declared they'd all been killed—only to discover a few days later a fresh horde of warrior weeds attacking "Green Pastures."

Weeds in my flowers!

And then there was that particularly vicious weed, I never did learn its name, that bloomed white in the fall but stayed camouflaged in the lawn the rest of the year. It had strong, steely roots. Long, stuck-tight roots. Roots that originated somewhere in China. Roots that passed all the way through planet earth to emerge in Oklahoma and explode all over our ground.

Weeds in my grass!

I hated that weed, that ever-expanding enemy of the yard. Ours was mostly hand-to-hand combat with me pulling with all my might and it holding fast in fixed position. I resorted to chemical warfare after a while. Even so, regardless of weapon or whatever I did, some days it seemed the weeds were winning.

Weeds in my flowers!

Weeds in my grass!

Weeds in my world!

"And Lord, I see more weeds in the world every time I open the newspaper. Dishonesty. Injustice. Bitterness. Selfishness. Backbiting. Cruelty. Lust. Greed. Row upon row of demonic weeds aggressively growing right in our midst.

"I see your people fighting them. Sunday by Sunday it's

51

'Onward Christian Soldiers.' But to be quite honest, Lord, it often seems the weeds are winning.

"And when your people fight until they're weary, and still the weeds appear to win—what then, Lord?"

The promise?

This poor man cried, and the Lord heard him, and saved him out of all his troubles. The angel of the Lord encampeth round about them that fear him, and delivereth them.

—PSALM 34:6-7, KJV

The answer?

I had fainted, unless I had believed to see the goodness of the Lord in the land of the living. Wait on the Lord: be of good courage, and he shall strengthen thine heart: wait, I say, on the Lord.

—PSALM 27:13-14, KJV

TWENTY-TWO
THE SOWER AND THE SEED

The haze in the early mornings. The chirp-song of the crickets. Autumn was in the air, and renewed optimism in my outlook.

It was now the last week in September and time to plant cool-season grass. I had been hearing about a Kentucky-31 tall fescue grass at the garden center. The manager there, a sweet older gentleman, told me it was a good, deep-rooted, vigorous grass that would grow in areas where Bermuda grass would not thrive. Fescue loves shade and clay soil, he said, so it should feel right at home in "Green Pastures." In fact, there were already a few clumps of fescue growing under the shady maple tree in the front yard. I decided to buy two pounds of fescue seed and fill in all the empty areas.

God took this opportunity to remind me,

Behold, the sower went out to sow; and as he sowed, some seeds fell beside the road, and the birds came and ate them up.
—MATTHEW 13:3-4, NASB

I poured the fescue seed into the whirligig seed spreader and began my seed-sowing trek across the yard. Oh, that Oklahoma wind! Some of my seed blew off the dirt and onto the driveway. Wasted seed. Happy birds.

And God said again,

And others fell upon the rocky places, where they did not have much soil; and immediately they sprang up, because they had no depth of soil. But when the sun had risen, they were scorched; and because they had no root, they withered away. —vv. 5-6

There was an area of bare dirt, carelessly walked on and hard as a rock, beside the driveway. I scratched some seeds into this hard-packed soil with my hoe. They sprouted earlier than the rest, and looked green for a week, but there was a high rate of casualties.

And God further warned,

And others fell among the thorns, and the thorns came up and choked them out.   —v. 7

There were two sections of lawn heavily infested with dandelions. I dug them out as best I could and then replanted those areas with fescue seed. But next spring the weeds were back, thanks to roots that had refused to budge, and the fescue there fought a losing battle with those bloomin' dandelions.

And others fell on the good soil, and yielded a crop, some a hundredfold, some sixty, and some thirty.   —v. 8

And yes, in those parts of our front yard where the ground had been well cultivated, and where the seedlings had been watered and fertilized at the right times in the right amounts, we had a bumper crop of fescue grass.

Why, we mowed our green grass at Thanksgiving while other people stayed indoors with their turkey dinners. And we mowed our green grass at Christmas while other people were inside wrapping presents.

We were still mowing our green grass at New Year's time when I heard a voice cry out from a passing car, "Stop fertilizing that stuff, or you'll just have to go on and on mowing it!"

Fertilizer?

Not much.

Mostly just fescue! And good old ground.

That winter our lush lawn was the talk of the town.

The lesson from the Master Gardener—

He who has ears, let him hear.   —v. 9

TWENTY-THREE
NO RAIN

Lord, no rain?
No rain again today?
I remember when it used to rain.
I see clouds on the horizon, hear thunder in my dreams—
Yet no rain.
No rain again today.
Such a dry, cold winter we had, and a dry, hot summer.
I ache for the feel of moisture in the air,
*   or the sound of raindrops on the roof,*
*   or the wondrous smell of a freshly-washed world.*
Oh, to see a rainbow in the sky!
But there is no rain.
No rain again today.
October leaves fall prematurely from the trees.
Browned, brittle, they fall in rattling heaps
*   on the hard, dry ground.*
No rich fall foliage this year—
And no rain, either.
No rain again today.
Lord, how burned and brittle we are
*   without your life-giving water.*
Lord Jesus—Water of Life to me—
*   there is no relief or salvation but in you.*

O thou that hearest prayer, unto thee shall all flesh come. . . .
Thou visitest the earth, and waterest it; thou greatly enrichest it
with the river of God, which is full of water. . . . Thou waterest the
ridges thereof abundantly: thou settlest the furrows thereof: thou
makest it soft with showers. . . . Thou crownest the year with thy
goodness; and thy paths drop fatness.

—PSALM 65:2, 9-11, KJV

Yet there is no rain.
No rain again today.

Wilt thou not revive us again: that thy people may rejoice in thee?
Shew us thy mercy, O Lord, and grant us thy salvation. I will hear
what God the Lord will speak: for he will speak peace unto his
people. . . . Surely his salvation is nigh them that fear him; that
glory may dwell in our land. . . . Yea, the Lord shall give that
which is good; and our land shall yield her increase.

—PSALM 85:6-9, 12, KJV

TWENTY-FOUR
THE YEAR IN REVIEW

The first frost was at hand. Harvest time. Time to evaluate what
had been accomplished this year in "Green Pastures."
    We had planted some flowers and seeded some grass. The
ligustrum did not live, but most of the other bushes had survived
our laying-on of hands. I think, considering our lack of know-how,
gardening went well for us—
except for the weeds,
and the webworms that wreathed the mimosa trees,
and the leaf rollers that tangled the redbud leaves,
and the leaf miners that tunneled the dwarf yaupon,
and the spider mites attacking the marigolds,
and there were aphids on top of the daisies,
and nematodes under the liriope,
and lace bugs in the pyracantha,
not to mention grasshoppers eating up everything else.
    Ah, the admonition of the Master Gardener;

Catch the foxes. . . . The little foxes that are ruining the
vineyards. . . .
—SONG OF SOLOMON 2:15, NASB

In gardening, as in life, little things mean a lot.

TWENTY-FIVE
A THORN IN THE FLESH

We had avoided the issue for weeks, my husband and I. Frankly, we didn't know what to say or what to do.

What do you do with thirty-nine old pyracantha bushes so overgrown that they invade neighboring yards, so overspreading that you can't walk around your property on two sides of your house, so overrun with lace bugs that they don't respond to your efforts to spray—and yet are so hardy that they constantly grow bigger and bigger?

We had been dealing with the pyracantha problem for a year, my husband and I. He on a ladder and I on a stepstool, our arms straining to reach into the thorny hedge with pruning shears and electric trimmer. Whoever named pyracantha "fire thorn" knew well the burn of its vicious barbs! We began our Saturday mornings with dedication and determination only to end up drenched with sweat, drained of energy, studded with thorns, and bloody.

And to think that such bloody Saturdays might stretch all the way from now until our dying days! In horror I visualized us in our eighties, still helping each other up the old ladder and stepstool, still struggling with the pruning shears and the hedge trimmer, still trying to keep the pyracantha walls neatly rectangular and crisply controlled. Did we really want to work that hard, and bleed that regularly, for the next twenty or thirty years?

One day, I remember it well, we finally had our fill of pyracantha. We said, "No more! No more trimming and spraying. No more problems for the neighbors. No more ladders and stepstools—and no more bleeding." Just the thought of a free Saturday now and then made us giddy with hope.

We phoned a friend who had a front-end loader. A tough, stout

58

vehicle that could squeeze into tight places between tree and fence and house and tree. A mighty-mite machine that could rear up on its back wheels and tear into a pyracantha bush with absolutely no bloodshed.

Our friend came over and went to work. With a heavy chain around a pyracantha trunk and a thunderous roar from the front-end loader, he pulled a monster-sized shrub right out of the ground, roots and all, in less than a minute.

Oh, that was a sight to see!

One bush. Two. Three. Ten. Twelve. Twenty—and the piles of pyracantha grew skyward like the pyramids of Egypt.

In no time at all, it was all over.

We were free at last of thirty-nine big old problems. No longer would our Saturdays be days of strain and pain. No more would we arrive at church with scratches in our arms and thorns in our fingers. Never again would I play "Safely through Another Week" on the Sunday school piano with a fire thorn in my thumb.

I know that some thorns-in-the-flesh never go away, as was the experience of the Apostle Paul. But ours went away on a front-end loader, and the last we saw of them they were buried in a landfill, never again to draw a drop of blood.

Thus says the Lord God, "Will it thrive? Will he not pull up its roots and cut off its fruit, so that it withers—so that all its sprouting leaves wither? And neither by great strength nor by many people can it be raised from its roots again."

—EZEKIEL 17:9, **NASB**

TWENTY-SIX
POSSIBILITIES I DID NOT PLANT

Thanksgiving Day was drawing near, and soon our extended family would be gathering at our house for the holidays. I kicked off my gardening shoes and put on my apron. Time for me now to work indoors, cooking and cleaning, getting ready for guests.

I started sorting out the contents of our kitchen cabinets and do you know what I found? Flower seeds. A special assortment of flower seeds sent by a friend who gardens in New Mexico. How long had this seed packet lain forgotten on the shelf? Nine or ten months at least.

I recalled the day the seeds arrived, how excited I was and appreciative of my friend's thoughtfulness. I would take good care of these seeds, I said to myself, so I put them away in the kitchen cabinet where they would not be spilled or scattered or lost.

And now it was November. And the carefully kept seeds were never planted—never given a chance to feel the comfort of soil or the warmth of sunlight or the wetness of rain. A few grains of potential, never invested or allowed their increase.

I paused in my housework to think about those seeds. I wondered what sort of plants they might have become and how their blooms would have looked last summer in my garden. Would they have done better than those bargain plants I bought that turned out so ugly? Would their blossoms have brightened both my yard and my spirit as each time I passed her love-gift and remembered my friend's kindness?

Would those plants have then produced seeds for still another season, seeds to share with others—an ongoing extension of a woman in New Mexico who cared about a garden in Oklahoma? Could I have given them to my married children to plant beside their homes—an expression of love from my generation to the next? A sharing of affection, gardener-to-gardener, from the heart and the hands of the Master Gardener?

"Well, Lord, the seed was never planted—and so it never grew—and thus I'll never know."

He who sows sparingly shall also reap sparingly.
—2 CORINTHIANS 9:6, NASB

TWENTY-SEVEN
WHAT TO DO IN WINTER

Before yard work changed for me from a dreaded chore to a delightful challenge, I thought of winter as a time to escape the great outdoors and go inside to sit by the fire. Wintertime was for thermal underwear and steaming hot chocolate, woolly-warm afghans and deep, deep sleep. People should hibernate like bears, I reasoned, until the cold winds of winter had blown themselves away.

But after gardening became my hobby, the dormant months took on new meaning. Of course, I still pulled on my long johns and wrapped up in an afghan while I sipped my hot chocolate—but now I discovered I could do all that and still carry on winter-weather gardening.

Oh, how much you can do in winter if you're a gardener!

You can evaluate last year's projects, see where you failed, and celebrate your successes.

You can mentally weed out what-to-discard from what-to-keep next season.

You can go back to your original design. What's been completed thus far? What changes are now needed in the five-year plan? What ideas have come to mind that could improve and accentuate your garden's unique beauty? How much will these new concepts cost, and can you afford them? Will these additions turn into problems for you ten years from now?

You may then draw up new plans to add fresh artistry for the coming months. Hang on to old values that served you well, but be open to new viewpoints that come with maturity.

And then you need to study to make your dreams come true. Gardening books, magazines, classes, incoming new spring catalogs. Don't overlook the seasonal notes you wrote to yourself all last year.

Sometimes you have to throw off the afghan, set aside the cocoa mug, get up from the easy chair, and pull on a coat to do your wintertime work.

It's a time to sharpen your blades, mower, and trimmer. While you're out there, oil your engines and grease your surfaces to keep your tools from rusting.

It's a time to thoroughly clean your sprayer of all pesticide residues.

It's a time to test your soil and assess its need for nutrients.

And sometimes you have to shape things, like that maple tree out front. Deep winter is the best time for pruning and reshaping many trees.

Sometimes you have to protect things, like newly-planted poppies. They should be warmly cuddled up in mulch while snoozing on the patio. But then there are other plants like irises and peonies that don't need a covering at all. Just like some babies sleep with their toes under blankets and some babies sleep with their toes hanging out, flowers also have individual needs.

Sometimes you have to prepare the soil to be soft next spring and not rocky. You can work up a sweat on a wintry day spading in peat moss and compost and gypsum.

And all along in the winter season you need to fight the enemy. Dandelions thrive in cold weather, I've noticed, and so do a lot of wicked old weeds. Come a sunny day with the wind slacked off, go spade up your garden and halt their invasion.

Another thing to do in winter is watch. Watch what's happening in your plants. Those bushes have a heart for spring long before we humans catch the fever. Go see how the buds on empty limbs are swelling and here and there have burst into bloom. They remind me of times I would put my children down for a long winter's nap. They would lie in their beds, blankets to their chins and eyes wide open, bodies bursting with impatience to pop out of bed.

"Can we get up now, Mommy?" they'd whisper.

"Stay down a little longer," I'd reply.

And now I seem to have that same conversation with bulbs and bushes as winter's chill ebbs and flows.

One more thing is needed—hope. Hope for tomatoes big as baseballs next summer. Hope for thick, green grass and fully-leafed trees. Hope for heavy-laden rose canes and a Persian carpet of flowery borders. Hope keeps you going on the coldest winter days. You'll need a lot of hope if you're a gardener like me!

EVALUATE—
  DISCARD—
    GO BACK TO THE BASICS—
      But add fresh beauty.
        Study, sharpen, purify.
          Test and revise.
            Protect and prepare.
              Wage war, watch and wait, and
HOPE! Oh, don't forget to hope.

And that's what to do in winter when January rolls around.

"Lord, was that my list of 'garden goals' or my 'New Year's resolutions'?

"Well, it'll do for both."

TWENTY-EIGHT
GRACE

It was easy to say good-bye to the pyracantha.

But the lilac bush was something else.

The first time I saw it, it was a skinny little shrub huddled up close to a crab apple tree. I don't know how long this lilac had lived there. It was not a promising location.

You can guess what I did. Of course you can! I dug it up and moved it to a wide open, sunny spot. And there it sits to this day.

But is it making any progress?

I give it water, fertilizer, mulch. Tender loving care.

It gives me tiny, tentative green buds—and little else.

I give it more fertilizer and mulch, more water, more care. I give it time. I give it grace.

But I don't plan on waiting forever for a bloom. Slow blooming is one thing, no blooming quite another.

Jesus once told this parable:

A man planted a fig tree in his garden and came again and again to see if he could find any fruit on it, but he was always disappointed. Finally he told his gardener to cut it down. "I've waited three years and there hasn't been a single fig!" he said. "Why bother with it any longer? It's taking up space we can use for something else."

"Give it one more chance," the gardener answered. "Leave it another year, and I'll give it special attention and plenty of fertilizer. If we get figs next year, fine; if not, I'll cut it down."

—LUKE 13:6-9, TLB

TWENTY-NINE
BITTER FRUIT

The Lord God, the divine Master Gardener, also evaluates his plants periodically:

My well-beloved had a vineyard on a fertile hill.
And He dug it all around, removed its stones,
And planted it with the choicest vine.
And He built a tower in the middle of it,
And hewed out a wine vat in it;
Then He expected it to produce good grapes,
But it produced only worthless ones. . . .

"Judge between Me and My vineyard," [He said].

"What more was there to do for My vineyard that I have not done
* in it?*
Why, when I expected it to produce good grapes did it produce
* worthless ones?*

"So now let Me tell you what I am going to do to My vineyard:
I will remove its hedge and it will be consumed;
I will break down its wall and it will become a trampled ground.

"And I will lay it waste;
It will not be pruned or hoed,
But briars and thorns will come up.
I will also charge the clouds to rain no rain on it."

For the vineyard of the Lord of hosts is the house of Israel,
And the men of Judah His delightful plant.
Thus He looked for justice, but behold, bloodshed;
For righteousness, but behold, a cry of distress. . . .

Therefore, as a tongue of fire consumes stubble,
And dry grass collapses into the flame,

So their root will become like rot and their blossom blow away as
dust;
For they have rejected the law of the Lord of hosts,
And despised the word of the Holy One of Israel.
                                            —ISAIAH 5:1-7, 24, NASB

"Creator Lord, if this judgment were true of men in Old
Testament times, how much more so in my world in this present
age.

"I read the record of your honest evaluation of a vineyard, and
I shudder to think how you must feel this day as you review the
bitter harvest here on earth. You look for growth in righteousness
and justice, and instead you get another crop of grief.

"What will you do now, Lord?

"What sweeping changes do you plan for this vineyard in
which I live?"

THIRTY
SECOND DEATH

And God said,

For ground that drinks the rain which often falls upon it and brings forth vegetation useful to those for whose sake it is also tilled, receives a blessing from God; but if it yields thorns and thistles, it is worthless and close to being cursed, and it ends up being burned.

—HEBREWS 6:7-8, **NASB**

Again it is said in God's Word,

The axe is already laid at the root of the trees; every tree therefore that does not bear good fruit is cut down and thrown into the fire.

—LUKE 3:9, **NASB**

And again,

. . . autumn trees without fruit, doubly dead, uprooted . . .

—JUDE 12, **NASB**

I thought of last year's pansies beside the back door. Some of them grew into robust plants and bloomed all over themselves last spring. And some of them just sat on their root systems and didn't do a thing. I waited and waited as patiently as I could. I gave them ample time and the same good care I gave their vigorous brothers. Still they did not bloom.

One day in quick anger I jerked up the nonbloomers and threw them away.

If I could do that to unproductive pansies, how much more my Creator to his disobedient creation.

And God continues,

Now these things happened to them as an example, and they were written for our instruction. . . . Therefore let him who thinks he stands take heed lest he fall.

—1 CORINTHIANS 10:11-12, NASB

I thought of many pansies, some colorful with blue and purple and yellow petals. Some with absolutely nothing, and soon dead.

And I thought of Moses. I remember how God warned him to make sure that his earthly work corresponded to the heavenly pattern God revealed to him on the mountain.

In ways I scarcely begin to understand, earth reflects heaven as surely as the ocean reflects sunlight. There are physical and spiritual principles at work here that mirror the eternal truths of God. The writer of Hebrews says they serve as a copy and shadow of heavenly things. They are earthly copies of divine patterns.

For instance, a cecropia caterpillar—a mere wormy thing—enters a cocoon and appears to die. But after its "death" it emerges transformed, free, elegantly colored in subtle shadings, high-flying now with a five-inch wingspan. And this earthly process of making a winged masterpiece out of a worm goes on year after year, a commonplace event. Yet it speaks to me of resurrection. It pictures a heavenly principle in a born-again moth.

And, to me, discarded pansies and uprooted fruit trees, thorns and thistles and burned-over ground point to God's heavenly patterns—an earthly reminder of judgment to come.

THIRTY-ONE
MEMORIES UNDER GLASS

Once you start working in the yard, one thing leads to another and soon you're doing things you never planned to do.

I started out as a self-defense hedge-trimmer, and went on to discover a new hobby, that of growing flowers. And once the flowers started blooming, I had all those pretty petals to deal with. It seemed a shame to let them wither and die and fall to the ground. I wanted to remember them—colorful, joyful, fragrant, and fresh. I began to cut the loveliest of the blossoms—saving them for memory's sake—and to press the petals between the pages of telephone books.

And that's how I became a petal preserver as well as a hedge-trimmer and an amateur gardener.

In spring I pressed petals of crocuses, irises, roses and daffodils. Also there were sprigs of forsythia and spirea, lily of the valley and honeysuckle. As summer drew near I added peonies, daisies, morning glories, and petunias to my petal collection. And then came midsummer lilies, late-summer clematis, and fall chrysanthemums, along with delicate ferns and decorative grasses.

When winter came I had three bulging telephone books full of flower memories. Remembrances too dear to throw away. But what do you do with dead flowers?

One January evening I brought my massive phone books to the kitchen table. I assembled scissors, paper, glue, toothpicks, and tweezers. I found large scraps of dark velvet fabrics, and I trimmed them to fit a number of empty picture frames.

Then I laid the petals out carefully on the blank white paper and I played with the petals, forming them into interesting designs. A twig here. A petal there. I lifted the twigs with the tweezers; I moved the petals around with a toothpick. When the design finally seemed satisfying and complete, I painstakingly moved it piece-by-piece onto a velvet background, and lightly glued each petal and twig into place.

That's when another hobby came into being—making flower petal pictures. Memories under glass, framed in gold frames, now hang on our walls. They are reminders of God's goodness during our first year in "Green Pastures." I did not want to forget the conversation with God nor the lessons I'd learned out there in the yard planting and picking flowers.

Gardening.

Petal-picturing.

Two good hobbies.

Good? No, they're great!

Any hobby is great if it turns your mind and heart toward God.

Bless the Lord, O my soul,
And forget none of His benefits
Who pardons all your iniquities;
Who heals all your diseases;
Who redeems your life from the pit;
Who crowns you with lovingkindness and compassion. . . .

As for man, his days are like grass;
As a flower of the field, so he flourishes.
When the wind has passed over it, it is no more;
And its place acknowledges it no longer.

But the lovingkindness of the Lord is from everlasting to
*   everlasting on those who fear Him . . .*
To those who keep His covenant,
And who remember . . .

—PSALM 103:2-4, 15-18, NASB

THIRTY-TWO
ROOTS

A blue norther was approaching Oklahoma.

It was the third week of January. If ever the weather turns bitter cold in Oklahoma, it seems to do so during the third week of each new year.

I prepared for the coming storm by bringing a supply of logs indoors for the fireplace. I checked the pantry and refrigerator to make sure we had plenty of food on hand. The weatherman was predicting rain followed by sleet and snow. It might be days before I could drive to the market for groceries.

I did the things my neighbors were doing to protect themselves and survive winter's icy blast. But what about plants? What keeps them alive in the stormy cold winds?

Roots.

Roots are the unseen strength of their lives. Roots steady a plant and hold it in place. Roots draw in water and nutrients from the soil. Roots store up food.

I looked out the window. The wind was blowing hard. Winter's freezing fingers had already touched my flower beds. Here and there I saw mounds of blackened, frozen leaves. Violets and veronicas, daisies and day lilies, all were lying in lifeless heaps. But underneath were roots. If it weren't for those roots, they'd be dead.

Roots are part of God's plan for living.

For there is hope for a tree,
When it is cut down, that it will sprout again,
And its shoots will not fail.
Though its roots grow old in the ground,
And its stump dies in the dry soil,
At the scent of water it will flourish
And put forth sprigs like a plant.

—JOB 14:7-9, NASB

But not all root systems have equal strength. There are plants with roots that live for years; we call them perennial. But some roots live only two summers or so; we call them biennials. And some roots die in just one year's time; they are called annuals.

Plants need the right root system to have staying power.

People, too, have root systems. Strong root systems that can make it through a storm. Young Timothy, a New Testament lad whose holding-on power grew out of his family's faith, had sturdy roots.

I am mindful of the sincere faith within you, which first dwelt in your grandmother Lois, and your mother Eunice, and I am sure that it is in you as well.

—2 TIMOTHY 1:5, NASB

I thought of the prayer of the Apostle Paul:

I bow my knees before the Father . . . that He would grant you, according to the riches of His glory, to be strengthened with power through His Spirit in the inner man.

—EPHESIANS 3:14, 16, NASB

"He is speaking of roots, isn't he, Lord?"

So that Christ may dwell in your hearts through faith; and that you, being rooted and grounded in love, . . . may be filled up to all the fullness of God   —vv. 17, 19

"Lord, multiply my rootage and my fruitage."

THIRTY-THREE
SURVIVORS

Speaking of root systems, the roots I have come to respect the most are those of the common dandelion.

I have found I can do almost any mean thing to the topside of that plant, yet those roots keep on keeping-on. In a world of easy wilting and sudden death (true at least in my garden), the dandelion is a model of survival.

The low-down dandelion has a thick, central taproot that can extend as deep as three feet into the ground. Besides the big taproot there is a complex system of root branches. The little yellow flower on top is but the tip of the iceberg, so to speak. Being a perennial plant, dandelions pop up year after year after year, as long as some of the root system remains in the soil.

Dandelions received their name from the French *dent-de-lion*, meaning the tooth of the lion—a picturesque reference to the plant's tooth-shaped leaves. But I think those early gardeners who gave the weed its name had also developed a grudging admiration for this lionhearted warrior, and they gave it a name consistent with its aggressiveness.

Dandelions are dynamic. They grow with vigor in all sorts of soil from sea level to high altitudes. Originating in Europe or maybe even Asia, they have taken our land by a most effective blitz. Blooming from March until frost in Oklahoma—and even blooming year-round in more southerly regions—the plant produces, after the bloom, the familiar "blowball" a week or so later. The winds come along, as do delighted children, and blow upon the "blowballs," sending dandelion seeds flying in all directions on silken-silvery parachutes. When the seeds finally fall to the ground, up comes a new colony of bright yellow blossoms.

No wonder we gardeners feel we never make a dent in the ongoing advance of the *dent-de-lions!*

I've been tempted to give up and let the dandelions take over "Green Pastures." I could say I've learned to like yellow flowers in my grass—or that I've learned to eat dandelion leaves in my salad. I've been told a cook can brew coffee out of dandelion roots, and batter-fry the blossoms, and add the buds to omelets. Some old-timers boast they make dandelion wine. But I don't know how to do those things. I've been too busy fighting dandelions to learn how to fix them for dinner.

But this I do know: they are survivors.

"See you next spring," I say with a sigh.

Therefore my beloved brethren, be ye steadfast, unmovable, always abounding in the work of the Lord.
—1 CORINTHIANS 15:58, KJV

May we take as our spiritual pattern the long-lived dandelion.

THIRTY-FOUR
NOT IN MY GARDEN
YOU WON'T!

A person needs a strong heart to read a book on gardening.

Page after page the drama and mysteries unfold as bug and bacteria come face to face with a root or a fruit. Who needs the secondhand misery of a soap opera when you can read about smuts and wilts, scabs and blights, mildews and molds, not to mention hordes of hungry beasties devouring every green shoot in sight?

I read about root rot.

"Oh, I hope that doesn't happen to us."

I read about stem cankers.

"Oh, please, not that!"

I read about damping off.

"Yes, I confess, that did take place here."

And I read about the freeze-thaw action of winter weather on root systems, and how sometimes a plant is pushed right out of the ground.

"Now that's one thing that we don't have to worry about. Our plants will not climb up out of the ground. I know them better than that!"

But later on, when I went for a walk and happened to pass by the iris bed. Guess what? Behind my back and against my wishes our irises had done it. They had come right up out of the ground and were sitting there on top of the soil with their roots hanging out, naked as jaybirds.

Never say, "It won't happen in my family." You never know when your very own irises will expose themselves to the neighbors.

Do not boast about tomorrow,
For you do not know what a day may bring forth.
—PROVERBS 27:1, NASB

THIRTY-FIVE

THE PERFECT TIME

Another thing I learned the hard way—which is probably the most effective teacher—was this: There is never a Perfect Time.

Unfortunately, my husband and I fervently believed in the Perfect Time.

We waited for the Perfect Time to spray the lawn for weeds. We waited through too wet or too windy days when we could be at home. And we waited through just-right days when we couldn't be at home. The optimum spraying dates came and passed, and the yard never got its comprehensive weed treatment that year.

Yet still we held tightly to the concept of the Perfect Time. We continued to idealize it and to wait for it. In fact, we made waiting for the Perfect Time into an art form. Nothing much got accomplished, but our consciences were clear. After all, we were busy—busy waiting for the Perfect Time.

We waited for the Perfect Time to spray with dormant oil— and the Perfect Time to cut back the clematis—and the Perfect Time to root prune the wisteria.

And then one day something amazing happened. We were moving some bushes around (doesn't everybody?) and transplanting them to better locations. It was a cool day late in winter, not exactly Perfect Timing but close. The cool day became a cool and cloudy day. Then it began to rain. But we kept on working. Then it began to snow. But we kept on working. And then we got wet and muddy and cold and snowy—but we kept on working.

And we laughed. Laughed at the snow and the mud and the cold. Laughed at how silly we must look to the neighbors. Laughed at how much we accomplished in such an un-Perfect Time.

It may surprise you to learn that all those dozen or so bushes took root and actually are growing now into fat, bush beauties. And it wasn't at all the Perfect Time to have a success like that!

King Solomon said it so well:

If you wait for perfect conditions, you will never get anything done.
—ECCLESIASTES 11:4, TLB

THIRTY-SIX

A GARDEN WEDDING

A funny thing happened on the snowy, muddy, laughing day we moved the bushes around in the cold.

Picture the scene. There were piles of castoff branches, pruned from shrubs, scattered haphazardly around our working area. Besides the branches there were garden tools, trash sacks, and garbage cans overflowing with still more discarded branches. We had begun our work that morning in an orderly manner, but as the day progressed, orderliness gave way to haste and chaos in the worsening weather.

When finally all fourteen bushes were safely planted in better locations and all the tools and trimmings put away, we found left on the lawn two root systems with a few inches of stem still attached to each one. No leaves for identification. Just two stems clinging to two chunks of roots. And they looked like such healthy roots that it grieved me to throw them away.

But which shrubs did they belong to?

Of the fourteen bushes we'd moved, there were six different kinds—viburnum, spirea, mock orange, forsythia, Japanese quince, and yellow leaf privet. Yet these two root chunks looked so similar, it would seem that they came from the same type of plant.

As I stood there shivering in the snow and the mud and the cold, pondering the problem of leftover roots, I thought of one more empty place in our yard that might be improved by the presence of a bush.

"Let's just stick these two roots in that spot over there," I said to my muddy husband. "They probably fell off the same bush. They certainly look just alike. We won't know until spring exactly which bush they came from, but if they survive we'll have an added bonus from our labor here today—plus a cheap way to fill in that empty spot."

So we stuck the two roots into the ground, side by side in the muddy clay.

It was some time later that bits of green began to appear. Slowly but steadily some twigs began to form, and on the twigs leaves began to sprout. Here a little leaf, and there a big leaf. A most unusual plant with small, dainty leaves and larger, broader leaves all growing quite contentedly together.

"Look here, honey," I said to my husband much later. "Those two chunks of roots must have come from two different shrubs. One with little leaves, and one with big leaves. Should we let them continue like that? I guess we ought to choose one or the other of the root systems and throw the leftovers away."

But when I checked beneath the branches, the enlarging system of tiny roots was so inextricably entwined it was impossible for me to separate them without killing both plants.

"Let's go ahead and let them grow together," we decided. "They've become almost like husband-and-wife. It would be a shame now to tear them apart."

And that's how our unique Raymond-Barbara bush was born. It's an eye-catching combination of bridal-wreath spirea and snowball viburnum, two deciduous six-foot shrubs. The viburnum grows around the base and sides of the bush, and bears large leaves and white blossoms as big and round as snowballs. Its mate, the spirea, grows up through the center of the shrub, its branches covered with tiny leaves and white flowerets more like snowflakes than snowballs. United, the airy, arching spirea branches flow like a fountain over the viburnum base. Together, the two plants are more interesting than either of them alone.

Uprooted together, painfully pruned together, yet growing and blooming together. So happy together I would not want to pull them apart.

"Looks like they've made a good marriage," I said to my husband.

We stood there studying the companion plants now reaching out and filling in the once empty spot in the landscape. Then my husband slipped his arm around my waist and gave me that loving squeeze I've treasured for thirty years.

"A very good marriage indeed."
And God said,

For this cause a man shall leave his father and his mother, and
shall cleave to his wife; and they shall become one flesh.

—GENESIS 2:24, NASB

THIRTY-SEVEN
THE UPWARD CALL

Brrr! Cold! I wrapped my coat more tightly about me, tied the belt firmly, and walked out the front door on my way to work. I started down the sidewalk, carefully avoiding the slushy snow lying gray and muddy on the lawn. The sidewalk, the street, the neighborhood, the sky—all were gray this wintry morning.

But then there was color, too. Springlike color! I was startled to see a drift of blossoms, sunshine-yellow and refreshingly bright, look up at me. What in the world?

Crocuses!

Then I remembered. I'd planted them a long time ago, back when there was warmth and blue skies and green leaves and soft breezes, and then I'd forgotten them. Indian summer gave way to cooler days, and winter arrived. The leaves of autumn fell in heaps above the crocus bed, and the winds of winter piled snow over their resting places. In the oncoming storms I forgot all about crocuses.

But the crocuses did not forget.

They did not give up on growing in spite of the heavy burdens above them and the icy circumstances about them. Imprisoned, forgotten, they held on to hope and to God's promise of spring, even during the darkest days of winter.

"Tiny bulbs, you are twice blessed. You bloomed where you were planted, as the old saying goes. And also, you kept your commitment to spring while still in the very grip of opposing forces. You kept on, and kept on, and kept on listening to that silent upward call.

"Welcome to my February world!"

I press on toward the goal . . . of the upward call of God in Christ Jesus.

—PHILIPPIANS 3:14, NASB

THIRTY-EIGHT
SIGNS OF THE SEASONS

I was clearing the table after a late supper. Glancing out the kitchen window I was surprised to see the sun still shining.

Supper is over, I mused, *and it's still so bright outside, even at this hour. Days are getting longer.*

"Good to see the sun, Lord!"

The cold winds still blew through Oklahoma's grasslands and now and then a cold front would blanket us in snow. But then more and more days were sunny with gentle, warm breezes. I could go outdoors in a sweater and not feel chilled at all.

"I think we're ready for spring, Lord. Just look at that blue sky, and that wonderfully warm sunlight. Don't you agree it's time for a break?

"The tips of daffodils are poking through the dirt. They are bursting their buttons to come up and bloom. Everywhere I look I see signs of new life. Time for a change—and I can feel it coming!"

And he said.

Now learn a parable of the fig tree; when her branch is yet tender, and putteth forth leaves, ye know that summer is near.
—MARK 13:28, KJV

And again he said,

When it is evening, ye say, It will be fair weather: for the sky is red. And in the morning, It will be foul weather to day: for the sky is red and lowering. . . . Ye can discern the face of the sky; but can ye not discern the signs of the times?
—MATTHEW 16:2-3, KJV

Weather forecasters and almanac writers and amateur gardeners, we know the signals for the changes in seasons.

But the clock of eternity—who can read its face?

The seasons of man—who can tell where we are?

THIRTY-NINE
WHO TAKES FIRST PLACE?

Just below our bedroom window we have three peony plants.
One blooms white, one blooms pink, and the third blooms a deep
rich rose. One nearly warm day I went outside to see if the
peonies had come up yet. A favorite flower, these peonies—and I
was eager to see them again.

Yes, they were up. Barely. Funny-looking, rosy-red shoots were
pushing up from the warming ground. But what were those green
leaves crowding in from all directions around the peony tips?

Daisies.

Oh dear, an inrush of daisies! I wondered if daisies and peonies
liked being such close roommates, sharing the same bed and food
and drink.

I went indoors and turned to the peony page in the gardening
book. And this is what I learned: when you plant peonies, you're
to plant them with the idea of leaving them in the same spot for
the next twenty years. You must not plant them near tree roots
or crowded up against hedges and bushes. You never force them
to compete with other plants for the nutrients in the soil. You
give them room, or else they decline.

I picked up a trowel and a spading fork, and I went back
outdoors to break the news to the roommates.

"Look here, some of you squatters are going to have to go.
Leave. Get out. There's not enough space here for both peonies
and daisies. One of you will take priority, and the other of you
will take the consequences. No spot can support two root
systems."

No one can serve two masters. . . .

It was Jesus speaking.

*Either he will hate the one and love the other, or he will hold to
one and despise the other. You cannot serve God and . . .*

—MATTHEW 6:24, NASB

God and something else.

One or the other has to go.

I dug out the daisies and replanted them in a space all their
own beside the patio.

And then it was time to set some other priorities in my life,
and thus to dig out all those something else's that sprout up like
daisies in early spring.

FORTY
IN THE GARDEN

It was March—at last! The dreary days of winter were forgotten as in a burst of fresh energy I tackled springtime tasks.

I was humming a melody as I anchored some rose canes to the fence. The song? It was "In the Garden."

C. Austin Miles was the composer of this hymn that has become one of the most popular gospel songs in our country. More than a million recordings were sold during the author's lifetime. It was written in March 1912 after Miles was inspired by reading his favorite chapter in the Bible, the twentieth chapter of the Gospel of John.

Mr. Miles was moved by the wonder of the scene John described—Mary coming alone to the garden tomb, early in the morning "while the dew was still on the roses," seeking to find the burying place of Jesus. As he thought of Mary on that first Easter morning, he imagined himself to be there in the garden with her when Jesus, the Master, appeared. What would it have been like to hear Jesus' voice call your name? To walk with him and talk with him? To be known by him on an intimate level of fellowship? What indescribable joy Mary must have felt!

The words of "In the Garden" fell easily into place as composer Miles put his mental picture on paper. Later that same evening he added the music, the same tune I hummed that March day.[*]

I wish I could have met Mr. Miles, author of three thousand hymns and editor of many collections of sacred songs. His friends say he looked like a southern colonel with a white mustache and

---

[*]George W. Sanville, *Forty Gospel Hymn Stories* (Winona Lake, Ind.: Rodeheaver-Hall Mack Co., 1943).

charming appearance. A witty and brilliant man, he wore a small, fresh flower in his lapel each day at his office. In his later years Mr. Miles often said he would make it through another year if he could get through the month of March.

He died March 10, 1946.

Jesus said,

If anyone loves Me, he will keep My word; and My Father will love him, and We will come to him, and make Our abode with him.
—JOHN 14:23, NASB

In the garden.

What better place to meet the living Lord?

FORTY-ONE
IMPATIENCE

"You've done what?" groaned my sophomore son. "You've bought 440 pounds of ———?"

He used an old family term, but I prefer to call it manure.

And yes, I did buy 440 pounds of manure one morning. I happily hauled it home, eleven forty-pound bags (all I could fit into my car) and began spreading it two inches deep around the root systems of my favorite plants. I wanted them to grow-grow-grow, fast-fast-fast.

In our instant-everything society, who has time for slowpokes?

Mercifully, the feed store clerk sold me manure rather than 440 pounds of commercial fertilizer. Talk about burnout or producing potential "type-A personality" plants! I learned later that if I had applied that many pounds of chemical fertilizer to so few plants, I would surely have killed them in my haste to hurry their growth. As it was, the manure had to decay before its nutrients could be available to the plants, and the decaying process took many weeks. Slow-acting and long-lasting, the manure in its own good time encouraged new growth and abundant blooms. Those were the lush results I longed for, but in my impatience could have spoiled so easily.

Instant growth? I no longer believe in it. Most good things take time—a good garden, a good arbor, a good character, a good marriage. The growing experiences of life are slow in their development. We rarely leap from trial to triumph without passing through a painfully slow process of maturing.

Spread all the manure you want—but it's still going to take some time before you can smell the roses.

Rest in the Lord and wait patiently for Him.

—PSALM 37:7, NASB

I waited patiently for the Lord;
And He inclined to me, and heard my cry.
He brought me up out of the pit of destruction,
*   out of the miry clay; . . .*
And He put a new song in my mouth, a song of
*   praise to our God.*

—PSALM 40:1-3, NASB

FORTY-TWO
HOLEY HOSES

Wind without rain. That was our weather forecast day after day.

My March garden had a thirsty look about it. Reluctantly I headed for the garden hoses, still wound in coils and rigid from the cold of winter. I took them out of the storage end of the garage and dragged them to the front lawn. Gently I tried to straighten them and lay them in long lines in the still-chilly spring sunshine.

"This first one looks OK," I thought to myself as I sorted them out. "But I think we ran over this other one with the car last fall. I see some cracked and damaged places in the plastic. And this third one—well, it is absolutely ancient. Maybe we ought to replace it this year. But then again, if it will work, why buy another one? I'll test them out and then decide."

One by one I hooked up the hoses to the outdoor faucet and turned on the water. One hose did its work well. The next one dribbled here and spurted there. And the third hose gushed fountains from a maze of cracks and holes.

One hose was immediately useful. One hose could be repaired. But that third hose? I considered what to do with it.

"Who needs a broken hose, Lord! Water is so important, so needed in any season. I've got to have a good source of water. But look at this hose—it's a sieve! It only wastes the water. . . .

"Water.

"How often you speak of water, Lord, when you describe yourself to us. You offer us *living* water in John 4:10, and from you flows a river of the Water of Life, pure, as clear as crystal.

"Water.

"To those who have gone dry you call out, 'Say there! Is anyone thirsty? Come and drink—even if you have no money!' "

Let the thirsty one come—anyone who wants to; let him come and drink the Water of Life without charge.

—REVELATION 22:17, TLB

For I will give you abundant water for your thirst and for your parched fields. And I will pour out my Spirit and my blessings on your children. They shall thrive like watered grass, like willows on a river bank.

—ISAIAH 44:3-4, TLB

"Water.

"You cry out to the crowd, If anyone is thirsty, let him come to me and drink. For the Scriptures declare that rivers of living water shall flow from the inmost being of anyone who believes in me.

"Water.

"And dry hearts do respond to you."

Come, let us return to the Lord. . . . Let us press on to know him, and he will respond to us as surely as the coming of dawn or the rain of early spring.

—HOSEA 6:1, 3, TLB

I looked at the brittle spikes of fescue grass and the desiccated leaves of thirsty evergreens. How great was their need for water.

O God, my God! How I search for you! How I thirst for you in this parched and weary land where there is no water.

—PSALM 63:1, TLB

A parched and weary land. Where there is no water.
I looked at the cracking soil.
I looked at the leaking hose.

The heavens are shocked at such a thing and shrink back in horror and dismay. For my people have done two evil things: They have forsaken me, the Fountain of Life-giving Water; and they have built for themselves broken cisterns that can't hold water!

—JEREMIAH 2:12-13, TLB

I stuffed the useless hose into the garbage can. Why put your trust in a broken cistern . . . ?

FORTY-THREE
RENEWAL

Saturday mornings now begin slowly at "Green Pastures."

After a hectic work week and nights spent in hospital hallways comforting yet another family through yet another crisis, my chaplain husband looks forward to sleeping a little later on Saturdays. And so we wake up slowly and get out of bed with delicious delay. We make a fire in the fireplace if the weather is chilly, and we pull our chairs up close. We brew a pot of coffee and share the morning newspaper. We talk and talk. We drink some more coffee—and talk some more talk.

But that Saturday wasn't our usual Saturday. A big event was taking place right outside our house, and I couldn't wait to get outdoors and watch it happen.

"Just look out there, honey," I urged my sleepy husband. "It's spring! The daffodils are up, and the forsythia's blooming. The sun is bright-shiny, and the south wind is warm. Let's go, and let's do something. Let's be kids again."

That Saturday we entered into spring!

That Saturday we flew a kite.

We stood in the empty field next to our property, and we sailed a rainbow-colored kite with a long rainbow-streamered tail high above our house. The soft yellow of the flowers, the soft green of the field, the soft blue of the sky, the soft flapping of the kite tail high above us in the soft spring breeze—I can still see it all, and hear it and smell it and feel it to this day.

"Have you ever sent a message on a kite?" asked my love. "I used to do it when I was a little boy. See, you get a piece of paper, tear a little hole in the center, and then slip the paper onto the string of the kite. Now watch what happens. See? The wind blows the paper up-up-up along the string—and the message finally goes clear up to the kite."

So we sent our messages and wished our wishes. We laughed off the weight of winter and played in the sunshine like children—like resurrected kids, alive again after a season of deadness.

My beloved responded and said to me,
"Arise, my darling, my beautiful one,
And come along.
For behold, the winter is past,
The rain is over and gone.
The flowers have already appeared in the land;
The time has arrived for pruning the vines,
And the voice of the turtledove has been heard in our land.
The fig tree has ripened its figs,
And the vines in blossom have given forth their fragrance.
Arise, my darling, my beautiful one,
And come along!"

—SONG OF SOLOMON 2:10-13, NASB

FORTY-FOUR
THE QUALITY OF MERCY

I remember the first time I fell in love with a flower.

I was four years old.

My parents had lived in various small cities in Texas, renting apartments for twelve years after their marriage. Now, at last, they could finally afford to buy a house. Mother's best friend, Mabel, and her husband were also wanting a new home. Together the two couples bought adjoining lots in the woodsy suburbs of a small town in east Texas and built almost identical houses next door to each other.

That first winter in our new home was such fun to me. I liked the trees around us and the open fields beyond. I liked the freedom of running over to our neighbors' house to see how Mabel and her husband were getting along. Our houses and our lots were as one big home to me.

One day in early spring I was on my way to Mabel's house when suddenly I noticed there was something special about her yard. Golden yellow flowers had somehow appeared and were lining her sidewalk all the way up to the front porch. A breathtaking sight to me! I'd never seen flowers there before alongside Mabel's walkway. And nothing so golden and spectacular had ever appeared in our yard. Where did they come from? What made them that color, or stood them up that straight? I couldn't wait to tell Mabel what had happened to her yard.

Tell her. No, I would show her. This flower miracle was too wonderful for mere words. So I picked every single flower—every one of Mabel's prized jonquils she had planted the fall before which would not bloom again for a full year—and hurried to ring her doorbell and give her this great surprise.

Fifty years of memory have not blurred the pained look on

Mabel's face as she came to the door and found all her precious jonquils snatched up from her yard and squashed into a bouquet by childish hands. Mabel had never had a child. She was a middle-aged matron who had saved her pennies through the long depression years, hoping for a house of her own someday, a house around which she could lovingly plant flowers.

I remember her just standing there in her doorway for a very long time, looking strangely unlike herself and saying not a word. At last she smiled and invited me into her house, kindly—the way she always did when I rang her doorbell. I recall she suggested we put the pretty flowers in a big, white vase. Together we filled the vase with water and arranged the bruised bouquet. How she kept from killing me on the spot I'll never know!

In time Mother sat me down and with grim face and stern words gave me a lesson on "Don't Pick the Posies in Other People's Yards." I have managed to restrain myself at the sight of a flower most of the time since then.

But I still love spring-blooming bulbs.

I dedicate this year's bulbs to you, Mabel. My golden daffodils remind me of your jonquils. I thank you for planting flowers so long ago to beautify your new neighborhood. I thank you for the happy memories and the kindness I found in your Christian home. I thank you for the mercy you bestowed on a neighborhood four-year-old, who still remembers your sweet spirit.

Here's to you, Mabel, with deep appreciation.

Who can find a virtuous woman? for her price is far above rubies. . . . She openeth her mouth with wisdom; and in her tongue is the law of kindness. . . . Her children arise up, and call her blessed.

—PROVERBS 31:10, 26, 28, KJV

FORTY-FIVE
SPRING FEVER

I was not the only one who felt the coming of spring.

In the supermarket and the dime store, racks of seed packets began to appear. Men and women, hurrying through their shopping lists, dashing up and down the aisles, would see the seed racks, hesitate in their hurrying, and finally stop a moment to look over this year's stock. I was no exception.

But what to buy?

What about petunias?

I wanted something colorful. Something that would spread out wide and handsome. Something local bugs didn't like. Something easy to care for that could stand up to heat and wind. Something that would bloom in a frenzy from now until November. Something that would stay healthy and lovely without asking too much of me.

So I looked for a petunia packet labeled "No perspiration needed."

I passed by the field of the sluggard. . . .
And behold, it was completely overgrown with thistles,
Its surface was covered with nettles,
And its stone wall was broken down.
When I saw, I reflected upon it;
I looked, and received instruction.
"A little sleep, a little slumber,
A little folding of the hands to rest . . ."

—PROVERBS 24:30-33, NASB

"OK, Lord, I get the picture.
No labor, no loveliness.
No persistence, no petunias."

97

FORTY-SIX
DYING TO LIVE

Jesus said,

Truly, truly, I say to you, unless a grain of wheat falls into the earth and dies, it remains by itself alone; but if it dies, it bears much fruit.

—JOHN 12:24, NASB

I wanted California poppies, so I planted some seeds.

An April rainstorm came along and flooded the flower border. I guess all the seeds sailed home to California, because I never saw them again. Not one poppy came up.

I wanted a morning glory vine, so I planted some seeds.

But the seeds never softened, never let their armor crack. They never put down a root or put up a leaf. Not one morning glory trumpet ever greeted the dawn.

"Lord, these seeds are not cooperating with me. They don't seem to see beyond the immediate moment. They rush away AWOL, or else they stay hard as rocks and just as lifeless.

"If they continue to resist like this, how will they ever come into bloom?

"Don't they know they won't succeed until they're ready to surrender?

"Don't they know they have to die before they can truly live?"

And Jesus said,

Whoever seeks to keep his life shall lose it, and whoever loses his life shall preserve it.

—LUKE 17:33, NASB

If anyone wishes to come after Me, let him deny himself, and take up his cross, and follow Me.

—MATTHEW 16:24, NASB

And I wondered, *Lord, are we speaking of seeds—or of me?*

FORTY-SEVEN
SURPRISE!

That spring I could hardly wait to see what would start to grow.

Maybe experienced gardeners don't feel this kind of anxiety. Perhaps they remember where they planted what, and have confidence that the right things will come up at the right times. I had little experience and even less confidence. If anything I planted came up, it would likely be a surprise to me.

It was a red-letter occasion indeed when the wisteria vine came back to life and bloomed in purple profusion. We also celebrated the day the lily of the valley blades broke through the ground—and the day the veronica put forth fresh green leaves—and the day new life emerged from the columbine quarters.

Congratulations, roots! You did your job well!

But some things I definitely remember planting never did show up again. Where did the bleeding heart go last winter? And those miniature chrysanthemums called "Baby Tears"? Whatever became of that delicate fern my mother-in-law gave me from her luxuriant fern border in Dallas? Did all those roots just give up and die?

And some things came up that spring that I never wanted to see again. That tough, tenacious weed I had spent two full days last fall digging out of the lawn—it came up. And the dandelions—they came up. I hoped I had conquered those unsightly weeds. I had dug up enough foliage to think I had defeated them. But I guess all their roots were never eradicated.

If something is alive down there in the hidden places, it's bound to come out sooner or later.

Now I know!

He who sees into those dark and hidden places said,

The root of the righteous yields fruit.

—PROVERBS 12:12, **NASB**

. . . if the root be holy, the branches are too.

—ROMANS 11:16, **NASB**

God again spoke of the power of roots:

See to it . . . that no root of bitterness springing up causes trouble, and by it many be defiled.

—HEBREWS 12:15, **NASB**

. . . lest there shall be among you a man or woman, or family or tribe, whose heart turns away today from the Lord our God . . . lest there shall be among you a root bearing poisonous fruit . . .

—DEUTERONOMY 29:18, **NASB**

A root bearing poisonous fruit.
A bitter root, springing up to cause trouble.
A righteous root.
A holy root.
They grow side by side in "Green Pastures."

FORTY-EIGHT

THE LIGHT OF THE WORLD

How we earth creatures rejoice each spring at the return of bright sunlight and warm weather!

Our planet is so far away from the sun that we receive only one two-billionth part of the sun's light and heat. Yet what an enormous difference this fraction of the sun's light and heat makes in our lives as we cycle from season to season.

Without sunlight ours would be a dark, dead world. An icy night would surround and entomb us, making life impossible.

No wonder God said it was good when he created light. The light of the sun is ablaze with his goodness. It touches earth with warmth and beauty, giving us color and radiance, giving us life itself.

I am the light of the world; he who follows Me shall not walk in the darkness, but shall have the light of life.

—JOHN 8:12, NASB

I have come as light into the world, that everyone who believes in Me may not remain in darkness.

—JOHN 12:46, NASB

Without the sun our planet would be a hungry world. Plants must have the sun's radiant energy in order to manufacture food. When the sun shines, plants respond by taking sunlight, water, and carbon dioxide and making them into sugar. Men and animals eat the plants and change the sugar and plant tissues into body tissues and bodily energy. Thus, when we eat plant food—or when we eat meat from animals who feed on plants—we are eating stored sunlight. And it is good.

102

In Him was life, and the life was the light of men.

—JOHN 1:4, NASB

As the sun shines longer and warmer each day upon my garden, I watch the plants respond. Up, up, up the seedlings are pulled as if by invisible strings. A tiny bulge on a stem soon becomes a leaf, and one leaf leads to another until there's a leafy wreath around the plant. Then come flower buds, followed soon by blossoms, as the plants grow higher and wider in response to the sun.

The Lord is my light and my salvation.

—PSALM 27:1, NASB

Spring is the busiest time of the year for me and my garden. Yet even on busy spring days I need to stop and remember where light comes from, and strength for growing. Too easily we busy people assume we can meet our own needs. We can keep ourselves warm, find our own food, light our own pathway. In this respect flowers are so much wiser than people. They know where to find abundant life—and it is not all within themselves.

They turn their faces up to God.

For with Thee is the fountain of life;
In Thy light we see light.

—PSALM 36:9, NASB

Someday we won't need sunlight any more.
But we'll never, ever outgrow our need of the Son.

No longer will you have the sun for light by day,
Nor for brightness will the moon give you light;
But you will have the Lord for an everlasting light,
And your God for your glory.

—ISAIAH 60:19, NASB

FORTY-NINE
WHEN NIGHT COMES

From the time of creation our earth has been rotating. Around and around. Day and night.

Then God said, "Let there be light"; and there was light. And God saw that the light was good; and God separated the light from the darkness. And God called the light day, and the darkness He called night. And there was evening and there was morning, one day.

—GENESIS 1:3-5, NASB

As we circled the sun, all living things on our planet have learned to be under an alternating pattern of light and darkness. Day and night, nicely balanced.

It is a lesson we all must learn.

As for plants, whether indoors or outdoors, almost every aspect of their lives—from seed germination to the eventual death of the plant—is under the rhythmic control of day and night patterns.

Not all plants live by the same patterns. Each species has its own daily rhythm involving fluctuations in root growth, in shoot growth, in water usage and so on. Like people, many plants have patterns based on a twenty-four-hour time period. But other plants prefer other rhythms. Night owls and sleepyheads in the same garden.

But what if a gardener could offer a plant unlimited sunshine? No more darkness. No more night. Wouldn't the constant daylight push the plant to reach its fullest growth?

No.

I was surprised to learn that most plants need times of darkness as well as light for normal development. Deprive them of their night, and they become unhealthy, damaged, scarred.

For example, if I tried to grow tomato plants in a constant blaze of brilliant sunlight, those plants would not grow as well or even weigh as much as tomato plants grown with a normal night-and-day pattern. Constant sunshine would make the leaves small, stiff and yellow, and they'd be scarred with dark spots where much leaf tissue had died.

I was even more surprised to learn that some plants have their maximum growth spurt in the middle of the night—and other plants toward the last hour of darkness. In the middle of their sunny day, however, they scarcely grow at all.

Darkness and light.

Day and night.

The rhythm of life that God says is good.

"Good, Lord? I seem to want all my hours to be sunny ones. If shadows fall across my pathway, my prayers are for you to take away this darkness and bring back the light.

"And when periods of deepest gloom come along, I cry out that this is not fair—this is not good—this blackness will hurt, will hinder fruition.

"Can it be that, like soybeans and henbane and other night-growing plants, I too will do my greatest growing when the moments are the darkest?

"And Lord—I fear to ask you this question, but a decade of heartache prompts my hunger to know—what if the darkness lasts a long time? For all those hours I've known of sunny pleasures, what if there is a corresponding balance of sunlessness when my world turns black and murky? Is this also a part of the pattern?

"And am I to go on going-on, even when I walk through a long stretch of night?

"What shall I choose to do when life is that dark?"

Bless the Lord, all servants of the Lord,
Who serve by night. . . .

—PSALM 134:1, NASB

FIFTY
CHOOSING A SPECIMEN

Something always seemed to be dying in my garden.

This time it was trees.

Actually, it was a freakish, twisting wind that took away most of the redbud tree in front of our house. We woke up one spring day to find our fences had blown down during the night and our redbud tree was twisted in two.

The three mimosa trees in the backyard weathered the windstorm. But then they began to die of the wilt.

We talked to the master gardener at the university extension center. We sought the counsel of nurserymen. All they could say was, "Your trees are dying. There is no remedy for wind or wilt. It's only a matter of time."

So we sadly cut the trees to the ground and dug out their roots. Their limbs eventually wound up as logs in our fireplace, giving us one last touch of color before ascending the chimney in smoke.

Now there were empty places in both the front and back yards. We missed the redbud, and we missed the mimosas.

"Shall we plant some more trees?"

We thought it over.

We decided we would.

Together my husband and I bought a booklet on trees and began to study the possibilities for replacement plantings.

"Here's a picture of a good-looking tree," said my husband, examining the booklet. "A pin oak. It says here that pin oaks grow tall and have a symmetrical shape. Dark green leaves in summer. Scarlet leaves in the fall. Excellent lawn tree, they say, but not suited for street planting."

"What about this southern magnolia?" I suggested as I scanned

106

the opposite page of the booklet. "I think they are the very essence of the South. Shiny dark foliage, with creamy white flowers, and the flowers smell heavenly. But it says here that the tree needs a great deal of space in which to grow, and the lower branches are supposed to be left untrimmed, touching the ground."

Page after page we read about the many different trees that could be planted successfully in our kind of soil in our part of Oklahoma. Each one was different in color, shape, size. Each had different requirements, different virtues and different drawbacks.

"Just what do we want in a tree?" my husband asked at last.

"Well, to replace the redbud tree in front," I began, "I'd like something airy-looking that won't hide our house from view, but leafy enough to shade the fescue grass below. It will have to be small enough to fit under the overhead utility wires. And I wish it would bloom some pastel color in spring, and then have berries or some rich fall foliage in October—in fact, something colorful each season that would blend with a red brick house."

"As for me," said my husband, "I want a tree or two in back that will add more shade to the patio. Maybe two tall trees, but wide enough to give us a sense of privacy. And no low limbs. We have to be able to walk under those trees in order to reach the back half of our lot. And—I've just thought of this—we've got to make sure we don't plant any trees where their roots will clog up the sewer line."

"Let's find trees that don't have to be sprayed as much as we had to spray that redbud," I added, remembering the leaf rollers.

"And let's hope the new trees don't drop seed pods all over the place like those mimosas," sighed my husband, remembering the nuisance of mimosa droppings.

The more we read and planned and dreamed, the more it became clear to us that we needed to find some very special trees to meet all our requirements. The tree for the front yard needed to be quite different from whatever we planted in the backyard. Obviously, the search for the just-right trees would take more time than we first anticipated.

Choosing the just-right individual, finding the perfect specimen, is it ever an easy task?

My thoughts turned to Jesus and his choices of "specimens." It was up to him to choose just the right individuals to place in leadership positions in the early church so that his work might succeed down through the centuries.

I remember how he chose the rough and impulsive Peter, a former fisherman, and gave him a task—"Shepherd my sheep." And then Jesus picked a different specimen of man, a "Son of Thunder" sort of fellow named John, to care for his mother Mary and write remarkable books and do other things in church leadership—tasks Peter was not suited to do.

Peter and John.

Yet when Jesus was about to depart and leave church leadership in their hands, when all of Christian history was riding on their shoulders, Peter got sidetracked. Sweeping aside his own personal responsibilities to Jesus, Peter decided to focus his attention upon John and to debate with Jesus the responsibilities of John.

Lord, and what about this man?

—JOHN 21:21, NASB

Jesus wasted no words in setting Peter straight.

If I want him to remain until I come, what is that to you? —u 22

If Jesus wanted John to stand right there on that spot until he took root, year after year after year until his final coming, it was not any of Peter's business. John was to be John and carry out Jesus' commission. Peter was to be Peter and do the things assigned to him by the Lord. Each leader was to be his unique self, God's specially-chosen specimen.

Choosing the just-right individual or specimen—is never an easy task. We are still in the process of seeking the right tree for the front yard (shall we call that tree Peter?) and a different but right tree for the backyard (shall we call that tree John?). They'll have to be different from each other in order to accomplish different purposes in differing environments. No clones need apply for these positions.

If our Peter-tree ever starts envying John and growing tall in imitation of the John-tree, we're in big trouble with the utility company.

We have many members in one body and all the members do not have the same function. . . . And since we have gifts that differ according to the grace given to us, let each exercise them accordingly.

—ROMANS 12:4, 6, NASB

FIFTY-ONE
A FAMILY TREE

In mid-life I discovered the hobby of gardening. My cousin Peggy, on the other hand, found a different mid-life interest. She became a genealogist.

From time to time Peggy wrote to me, sending new information she turned up about our family history. The pedigree charts grew longer and longer as Peggy fleshed out branch after branch of our family tree. What interesting individuals she found who had bloomed on our boughs at some point in history.

There was my grandmother Jennie who at age twenty-eight died suddenly in June, her birth month, leaving behind a grieving family including three young children. Her church met in session and passed a lengthy, beautifully written resolution telling how much young Jennie had meant to their body of believers. I hold a copy of the frayed, yellowed June 1908 resolution in my hands, and I marvel at the continuing influence of Jennie's short life.

There was John who, with two other Christians, started a little church in Alabama in 1819. They built their first house of worship with logs. From the rough-hewn church came so many young men answering God's call to service that it became known as "the cradle for ministers." In 1865 the church grounds became a Civil War battleground. The scars of bullets are still in evidence. Yet John's little church lived on to proclaim the Good News of the Prince of Peace to war-weary survivors in that part of the South.

There was Rebecca who brought a long-loved fruitcake recipe with her when she married into my family in 1788. To this day we enjoy Rebecca's recipe, although her baking instructions are a bit hard to follow using my electric oven:

Five sticks of wood for the first hour.
Four sticks of wood for the second hour.
Three sticks of wood for the third hour.
Two sticks of wood for the fourth hour.
One stick of wood for the fifth hour.
Then let the fire go out and let the oven door stay open until the
cake is cool.

I see a bit of Rebecca in my daughter, both of them skilled in
the arts of hearth and home.

And then there was sailor David, born in 1726, who invested
his energies in transversing the Atlantic Ocean. He was master of
a sailing ship that made rounds from England to America and
back. Sailor David's interests—and maybe his genes as well—live
on in my sea-loving son.

But along with the blossoms on the family tree, we've had our
share of blight.

We read in dismay of the slave owners who passed human
property to their children in their last wills and testaments. How
can a man possibly own his fellowman? The thought of it sickens
our family now.

Blight and blossom, and thus the centuries pass in review. In
each generation we've added new interests and new names "for
better or for worse" to the limbs of our family tree. My husband's
name now joins mine, and below our names come the names of
our three children, their spouses and their children.

By inward growth and outward grafting, the tree spreads and
casts an increasing longer shadow.

"So many new names, Lord! All this grafting and growing
needs to be put into an expert's hands. A family tree is too
important to be placed in the care of amateurs.

"Will you watch over this enlarging family structure, and keep
it true to you?"

And Jesus said,

*Abide in Me, and I in you. As the branch cannot bear fruit of itself
. . . so neither can you, unless you abide in Me. . . . He who
abides in Me, and I in him, he bears much fruit; for apart from
Me you can do nothing.*

—JOHN 15:4-5, NASB

FIFTY-TWO
A HEALTHY DOSE OF DOUBT

There are experts and there are experts.

It pays to find out which is which.

Once there came to our door a couple of men in work clothes who said they were tree-trimming experts. They drove a pickup truck and carried an assortment of tools. They were friendly and available, and their price fit our budget. It seemed that the deal they offered was a good one—until I observed their work.

I checked to see how they had trimmed the trees on neighboring streets before they worked their way to our block. Tree-trimming? I'd say tree-torture. Mutilation. I stared at those hacked-up trees in horror and thought that turning those men loose on our maple tree would be like asking a butcher to groom our dog.

Not everybody claiming to know really knows.

Thou shalt not be gullible.

Thus says the Lord of hosts, "Do not listen to the words of the prophets who are prophesying to you. They are leading you into futility; . . . Behold, I am against those who have . . . led My people astray by their falsehoods and reckless boasting; yet I did not send them or command them, nor do they furnish this people the slightest benefit."

—JEREMIAH 23:16, 32, NASB

Now I'm learning to spray all expert claims with a healthy dose of doubt.

It gets rid of a lot of false prophets and pests.

FIFTY-THREE
PICKING AND PINCHING

There are appropriate methods to trim off excess baggage on a plant.

Sometimes you should "pick."

At other times you should "pinch."

"Picking" is the removal of faded, ruined blossoms in order to stimulate the plant into new flowering. Throughout the blooming season many plants such as carnations and pansies, feverfew, and petunias, will profit from their flowers being picked day by day.

"Pinching" refers to cutting out a portion of the center of single-stemmed plants when they are young, in order to make them grow stockier and bushier. On tall, leggy plants you pinch off three or four sets of upper leaves just above a leaf axil. This stops upward growth and forces the plant to produce side branches directly below the pinch point. Not only does this treatment encourage better branching, but also better flowering. Mums, dahlias, snapdragons, and asters, among others, benefit from being pinched.

The first time I ever pinched a plant I feared I would kill it. Picking off faded blossoms was one thing, but pinching back a brand new petunia I'd just bought? It seemed a mean thing to do to a young bedding plant as well as financially irresponsible. I'd just paid a quarter for the little fellow—and then to pinch him in half and toss away the top? Toss away the better-looking end?

Yet getting rid of its excess baggage helped my petunia plant grow into a bushy, well-developed bloomer. As its blossoms faded and hung at half-mast on the stem, I then picked off and discarded its past glories in order to conserve and focus its energy toward future flowers. It bloomed like crazy all summer long.

I've learned it comes down to this: Do you look backward to the past or forward to the future?

Yesterday's petals become dead weight today.

Tomorrow's blooms are worth the pain of picking and pinching.

One thing I do: forgetting what lies behind and reaching forward to what lies ahead, I press on. . . .

—PHILIPPIANS 3:13-14, NASB

FIFTY-FOUR

THE YEARS THE LOCUST HAS EATEN

Do not fear, O land, rejoice and be glad,
For the Lord has done great things. . . .
For the pastures of the wilderness have turned green,
For the tree has borne its fruit,
The fig tree and the vine have yielded in full.

So rejoice, O sons of Zion,
And be glad in the Lord your God;
For He has given you the early rain for your vindication.
And He has poured down for you the rain,
The early and latter rain as before.

—JOEL 2:21-23, NASB

In May I drove through flooded streets in a torrent of rain to get to the garden center. Call it madness—call it cabin fever—it seemed the thing to do at the time. We needed some pesticides in order to face the oncoming pests—and in a rainstorm like this one, surely the checkout line would not be long.

The little old gentleman in the garden center remembered me from the summer before. I guess one can't forget a shopper who stands motionless for half an hour trying to choose between two shades of red impatiens. He welcomed me warmly. "Where have you been so long? You ought to drop in and see me in winter. It gets a bit lonesome around here in January."

Together we selected insecticides and fungicides and a sack of dusting sulphur. There were no other customers for him to serve. Then we tarried a few minutes at the front entrance and watched the rain come down in sheets. We spoke of winter's storms and the gale-high winds of March. He was hoping for a new shipment

115

of crape myrtle bushes soon—and had I noticed the new blue hollies out in back? I told him about the leafrollers and the leafminers, and how a bunch of aphids simply destroyed a clump of daisies. He told me how to clean the garden sprayer after use, and warned me not to dust with that sulphur when the weather turns hot in July.

Some sweet day the Lord will renew this earth and get rid of its pests and its problems forever. But until then, I'll keep a supply of bug spray on hand and enjoy the company of the little old gentleman who works at the garden center.

The promise of God encourages me:

Then I will make up to you for the years
That the swarming locust has eaten,
The creeping locust, the stripping locust,
  and the gnawing locust, . . .
And you shall have plenty to eat and be satisfied,
And praise the name of the Lord your God,
Who has dealt wondrously with you.

—JOEL 2:25-26, NASB

Only the Master Gardener can make all these things work together for good—as in Romans 8:28—or make up to his children for the years lost to the locust.

FIFTY-FIVE
A MUSTARD SEED

And He said, "How shall we picture the kingdom of God, or by
what parable shall we present it? It is like a mustard seed, which,
when sown upon the soil, though it is smaller than all the seeds
that are upon the soil, yet when it is sown, grows up and becomes
larger than all the garden plants and forms large branches; so that
the birds of the air can nest under its shade."
—MARK 4:30-32, NASB

"Lord, I am planting little seeds today in flats. They are such
little seeds. One has to believe in miracles to think something as
tiny as a fly-speck is going to grow two feet tall and a foot
wide—and maybe even bloom!"
And Jesus said,

If you have faith as a mustard seed, you shall say to this
mountain, "Move from here to there," and it shall move; and
nothing shall be impossible to you.
—MATTHEW 17:20, NASB

"Lord, remember the bracelet I used to wear, the one with the
mustard seed sealed up in a clear plastic charm? Someone gave
it to me as a gift. I used to wear that bracelet and think of you—
and wonder what in the world a mustard seed and God had in
common. *Were you at all interested in a seed?* I wondered.
"But a year of gardening has expanded my understanding. I
see with new eyes that a mustard seed can come alive. It's an
earthly speck of spiritual truth. The gospel in miniature. Good
News in small print.
"Such a tiny seed it is, Lord, yet loaded with power. It grows
in some places as tall as a horse and rider. A mustard seed in

fertile soil can become a ten-foot-tall shelter for birds. And mustard-seed faith can move a mountain!

"Nothing is impossible for you, Lord.

"And because of you within me, nothing is impossible for me, either.

"You can take a mustard seed and make it into a masterpiece. For you took a fisherman's faith and built an everlasting church. You took a little boy's lunch and catered a feast for five thousand men. You took a shepherd lad, the runt of the litter in the eyes of his family, and made him David, king of Israel, a conqueror of giants, a man after God's own heart.

"God of the mustard seed and me, here we are. Take us and transform us and make us into miracles."

FIFTY-SIX
SOMETHING OLD, SOMETHING NEW

One of the reasons English gardens are so appealing is their subtle blending of old and new. Look at the paintings of English landscapes and see the picturesque combinations of soft, misty-colored flowers framed by ancient stone walls.

In my Oklahoma gardening, I also seek to mix the new with the old. Delicate purple crocuses blooming beneath the massive old maple tree. Wispy blue columbine nestled beside a mossy old stone. Ruffled pink petunias clustered within the crooked angles of silvery old driftwood. New and old, balancing one another.

A family is like a garden. We are a mixture of youth and maturity, a blend of new and old. Grandparent, parent, child, grandchild—all growing together and giving balance to one another's lives.

. . . first the blade, then the head, then the mature grain in the head.

—MARK 4:28, NASB

The grandparent is the link to the family's heritage, and gives the group the needed perspective, stability, and good-natured patience to face the present age. How I treasure my husband's mother who has demonstrated time and again the character traits I aspire to have. How helpful has been her viewpoint, and how often we lean upon her wisdom.

The parent provides the nurture, the care-giving, and the counsel ("I'll help you fix the dinner . . . pay the bill . . . learn to drive . . . fill out the tax form . . .") for the younger generation and the older one as well.

119

The young-adult child has the strength and the energy, the daring and the dreams that keep family life progressive and exciting. "Look, Grandma, I bought a car." . . . "Look, Dad, I enrolled in college." . . . "Look, Mom, we're pregnant!"

And the grandchild? Ah, the baby's the hope and the joy and the fresh focus on tomorrow.

We meet each other's needs.

We need each other.

One generation shall praise Thy works to another,
And shall declare Thy mighty acts.

—PSALM 145:4, NASB

In Psalm 144 I find what seems to me a garden scene. A family is growing here. In my mind's eye I see young sons springing up straight and strong and stately. Like palm trees in Palestine. Like oak trees in Oklahoma. Among the trees and young budding plants are beautiful pieces of statuary. Feminine forms, curving and graceful. Daughters fitted for a palace, carved as for a corner pillar. And sheltering this peaceful place, I imagine an old stone wall, crumbling perhaps and weathered with age, but still providing protection and guidelines for all the tender growing things within its embrace.

Let our sons in their youth be as grown-up plants,
And our daughters as corner pillars
 fashioned as for a palace . . .

—PSALM 144:12, NASB

Grandparent, parent, child, grandchild.

A people garden.

How blessed are the people who are so situated;
How blessed are the people whose God is the Lord!   —v. 15

FIFTY-SEVEN
FRUIT IN OLD AGE

My mother has Alzheimer's disease. She has had it for a very long time. For the past seven years she has had to have the twenty-four-hour-a-day care of a nursing home. We celebrated her eightieth birthday this year.

This incurable disease has left her extremely brain-damaged. She lies in her bed drawn up into a fetal position, incontinent, mute, and scarcely able to move. She can open and shut her eyes and turn her head slightly and grip a hand if placed within her grasp, but that's about all. Except to smile. Even now, after all these years and all that brain damage, her smile can light up a sickroom.

Her roommates come and go as the years roll on. Some of them have improved and gone home; others have gotten worse and passed away. Many of them became cranky and bitter, foul-mouthed, and demanding in their later years. Mother just keeps on smiling. The nurses appreciate her sweet spirit. They in turn shower her with love.

Sometimes I wonder at the ways of God, and why it is he allows a brain-damaged Christian to go on living a bedridden life. She is his child! Why should she be here and helpless when she could be strolling the streets of heaven and serving the Lord she loves? What possible good can come from a life lived mute and motionless in a nursing home!

And then I see her smile and I see the happy, loving look in her eyes. And besides love I see joy and peace, patience and kindness, goodness, faithfulness, gentleness, self-control. All the fruits of the Spirit amazingly still being borne in a ravaged body and unguarded mind that long ago forgot the basic facts of life; like what day or year it is, and whether or not she has a family, or who she is and what might be her name.

Yet the Spirit within her still bears fruit.

I remember what she taught me about going to church a few years back—a lesson taught without words or gestures but simply by a look that came into her eyes. On my way to a worship service I had stopped by to see her. I happened to say in Mother's hearing, "I am on my way to church"—something I've said to her many times before and since, but the brain damage had never let my message reach her mind. This time, what I said got through the barriers. My words made connection and were comprehended.

For a moment her eyes grew wide with excitement and remembering, and then there came such a look of longing as I have scarcely seen in any face in all my life. Like a beggar remembering bread. Like a drowning man remembering breath. Wordlessly she communicated her feelings: "Church! I remember church! What a wonder to go to church!"

Her eyes held mine for a few seconds—I could not even breathe for their intensity—and then the doors of memory closed once more. She no longer remembered the word *church* and all it stood for, or even that I was her daughter and she my mother.

But I cannot forget.

Her lesson left its imprint upon my life.

To this day I do not enter a house of worship without remembering the look of longing in my mother's eyes. She clearly defined for me what is sacred and of surpassing worth. And she never said a single word.

God speaks of his fruit-bearing child this way:

His delight is in the law of the Lord; and in his law doth he meditate day and night. And he shall be like a tree planted by the rivers of water, that bringeth forth his fruit in his season; his leaf also shall not wither. . . .

—PSALM 1:2-3, KJV

And of his children in advanced years he says:

Planted in the house of the Lord,
They will flourish in the courts of our God.
They will still yield fruit in old age;
They shall be full of sap and very green,
To declare that the Lord is upright;
He is my rock, and there is no unrighteousness in Him.

—PSALM 92:13-15, NASB

Such a frail "planting" is my mother. Eighty years old and barely eighty pounds of skin and bone. But she is still bearing fruit and teaching her family to honor the Lord.

Her mind withered, but not her leaf.

FIFTY-EIGHT
HARVEST TIME

To my delighted eyes "Green Pastures" bloomed in exceptional beauty that summer.

The grass, once sparse and scratchy and full of weeds, now grew green and thick, as soft and bouncy under our bare feet as the puffy comforter on the grandbaby's bed.

The crab apple trees produced clouds of pink blossoms, and the maple tree grew upward and outward, an emerald umbrella.

The flowering shrubs were robed in yellow and white, bright coral, and soft mauve. The tomato plants hung heavy with fruitfulness, as did the canes of the red rambler roses. And oh, the vines—the purple wisteria and the creamy honeysuckle and the white Sweet Autumn clematis—they seemed in nose-to-nose competition as they spread their fragrances on the Oklahoma air.

And flowers? Like a rainbow of pretty colors circling our house, they bloomed from February until late November. Crocuses, of course. Daffodils and tulips. Lily-of-the-valley sprigs, and violets. Pansies and peonies. Daisies and gaillardias. Irises and lilies. Oriental poppies, petunias, periwinkles. Hollyhocks, columbines, cannas. Salvias and geraniums. Marigolds and ageratums. Veronicas, impatiens, and finally chrysanthemums. I could make floral arrangements for each room of our house, take a nosegay to the nursing home and another to my office, and still have flowers left over for making bouquets tomorrow.

But did our yard win some sort of award? Or look like an ad in a flower seed catalog?

Not at all.

Even an amateur plant-lover like me could see there was much room for improvement. There were wrongs to be righted, new diseases to diagnose, new bugs to battle, new weeds to work on, and new notations to make in my gardening book.

But we'd made a start, a fresh beginning. The bleak had become beautiful and bloomed all over.

This bountiful harvest—how did it happen?

Was it the sun and the rain that produced such a crop? Or the manure and the fertilizer and the carefully-maintained mulch? Was it the weeding and spraying, or the soil cultivation? Was it the sweat of our brows, or the tears in our eyes? Was it the sorrows we buried in our quarter-acre lot?

Was it all this and more?

An awesome act of God?

I only know that what was once a wilderness burst into bloom. And at the same time the barren places in my innermost being grew fertile and productive in the Master Gardener's hands.

Out of unanswerable questions and seasons of despair, out of sickness and sin and hurting and struggling, there came a joyful time of harvest.

And who but God could take a lump of clay and bring it into bloom as he did here in "Green Pastures"?

All discipline for the moment seems not to be joyful, but sorrowful; yet to those who have been trained by it, afterwards it yields the peaceful fruit of righteousness.
—HEBREWS 12:11, NASB

And the wilderness becomes a fertile field
And the fertile field is considered as a forest. . . .
Then my people will live in a peaceful habitation,
And in secure dwellings and in undisturbed resting places.
—ISAIAH 32:15, 18, NASB

FIFTY-NINE
CHANGE OF SEASON, CHANGE OF HEART

"Dear Lord, as I work here in my garden today, I attend to my tasks with fresh peace in my heart. The soft greens of the landscape are a reflection of the greening taking place in my innermost self. I feel refreshed, cleansed, hopeful, happy.

"I feel as though you've created a new me!"

For as the earth brings forth its sprouts,
And as a garden causes the things sown in it to spring up,
So the Lord God will cause righteousness and praise to spring
up. . . .

—ISAIAH 61:11, **NASB**

"Lord, I praise you for your faithfulness. You keep your word. Your promises are unbroken. You never fail."

While the earth remains,
Seedtime and harvest,
And cold and heat,
And summer and winter,
And day and night
Shall not cease.

—GENESIS 8:22, **NASB**

"Lord, I praise your mighty power. You create. You re-create. Winter becomes spring, and spring blooms into summer. Renewal takes place, without and within."

126

O Lord, how many are Thy works!
In wisdom Thou hast made them all. . . .
Thou dost open Thy hand, they are satisfied with good.
Thou dost hide thy face, they are dismayed. . . .
Thou dost send forth Thy Spirit, they are created;
And Thou dost renew the face of the ground.

—PSALM 104:24, 28-30, NASB

"Lord, I thank you for your loving care. You have provided for our personal needs—shelter, sustenance, healing, hope. You have given us . . ."

Beauty for ashes;
Joy instead of mourning;
Praise instead of heaviness.

—ISAIAH 61:3, TLB

"I hear your words as one Gardener to another:"

Observe how the lilies of the field grow; they do not toil nor do they spin, yet I say to you that even Solomon in all his glory did not clothe himself like one of these. But if God so arrays the grass of the field, which is alive today and tomorrow is thrown into the furnace, will He not much more do so for you, O men of little faith?

—MATTHEW 6:28-30, NASB

"I do not know, Lord, how you met my many needs. I only know that when each crisis came, you were there. And you were able. Every time."

The Lord sustains all who fall,
And raises up all who are bowed down.
The eyes of all look to Thee,
And Thou dost give them their food in due time.

—PSALM 145:14-15, NASB

"I do not know, Lord, how you will solve the problems that are yet to be solved. I only know you can. And you care."

A bruised reed He will not break. . . .

—ISAIAH 42:3, NASB

"To the bruised you bring healing. To the hopeless you bring change."

He changes a wilderness into a pool of water,
And a dry land into springs of water.

—PSALM 107:35, NASB

"Lord, this wilderness of mine—these years of pain and perplexity, all the whys that go unanswered—you have taken into your hands and made it a growing place. You change a wilderness to water!"

Happy are those who are strong in the Lord, who want above all else to follow your steps. When they walk through the Valley of Weeping it will become a place of springs where pools of blessing and refreshment collect after rains! They will grow constantly in strength. . . .

—PSALM 84:5-7, TLB

"You change a wilderness to water—and water to wine. You changed my wilderness—and you changed me.

"Thank you for caring that we come into bloom."

SIXTY
GARDEN PEOPLE

Men and women, boys and girls—we are all divinely designed to live in gardens.

In the beginning God created the heavens and the earth. . . . And God saw all that He had made, and behold, it was very good. . . . And the Lord God planted a garden toward the east, in Eden; and there He placed the man whom He had formed.
—GENESIS 1:1, 31; 2:8, NASB

Looking backward in time to the dimmest memories of human existence, we find man coming into being in a garden. He is formed of its dust. He breathes in its fragrance. He opens his eyes; he discovers a Gardener.

Then the Lord God took the man and put him into the garden of Eden to cultivate it and keep it. And the Lord God commanded the man, saying, "From any tree of the garden you may eat freely; but from the tree of the knowledge of good and evil you shall not eat, for in the day that you eat from it you shall surely die."
—GENESIS 2:15-17, NASB

A wondrous garden it was, designed and planted by God himself. And there was only one testing tree for God's people to leave alone.

Just one tree.

Just one.

But you know the story, as all of us do, for it is the story of all our lives. We fail the test and we go off course. We overstep the loving boundaries of God. We trample the tender limits of the Lord. And in so doing, we destroy our garden home.

129

Cursed is the ground because of you; . . .
Both thorns and thistles it shall grow for you; . . .
By the sweat of your face
You shall eat bread,
Till you return to the ground, . . .
For you are dust,
And to dust you shall return.

—GENESIS 3:17-19, NASB

So the Master Gardener, Lord of Eden, sent the man and his wife out of the garden, and stationed a guard to bar their return to the Tree of Life.

Yet even in the wilderness of thorns and thistles, sweat and dust, the fragrance of Eden haunted their memories. They were garden people in spite of their sin, but ever so far from home.

And then Jesus came, bearing about himself the lovely scent of Paradise. The Gardener—he was here again! Men called him by garden names. Rose of Sharon. Lily of the valley. The Branch. The Root out of dry ground. Men saw in Jesus the way back to Eden.

We are garden-needing people, in spite of our sin.

So we plant a little garden plot where we presently live. I plant mine in Oklahoma, you in your dwelling place. It blooms with a hint of what once was Eden, and our hearts feel strangely lonely for that long-ago homeland.

Men and women, boys and girls—we are all hungering for our garden birthplace. We may not label our hunger pang precisely or know its source, but we feel it continually, year in, year out. We expend enormous energies and staggering sums of money to appease the pain, to fill up the void. We decorate our wilderness, and we gild our thistles. Yet what we're really seeking is the contentment and peace Adam had in the beginning when he walked with God in the cool of the day.

But it will not always be this way.

Someday God's garden gate will again swing open to his people—and we shall return to our native land.

John, the apostle, the beloved "Son of Thunder," caught a glimpse of our future garden home. He describes it in these words:

I saw a new heaven and a new earth; for the first heaven and the first earth passed away. . . . And He who sits on the throne said, "Behold, I am making all things new." . . . And he showed me a river of the water of life, clear as crystal, coming from the throne of God. . . . And on either side of the river was the tree of life, bearing twelve kinds of fruit, yielding its fruit every month; and the leaves of the tree were for the healing of the nations. And there shall no longer be any curse. . . . And there shall no longer be any night; and they shall not have need of the light of a lamp nor the light of the sun, because the Lord God shall illumine them; and they shall reign forever and ever.
—REVELATION 21:1, 5; 22:1-3, 5, NASB

In the beginning—and in the beginning again—God's eternal purpose is that we should all be garden people, home with him, ever alive.

SIXTY-ONE
EVERYTHING SAYS GLORY

Holy, Holy, Holy, is the Lord of hosts,
The whole earth is full of His glory.

—ISAIAH 6:3, NASB

On these pages I have shared with you, dear reader, my
experiences of working alongside God in making a garden in
Oklahoma. I wish it were possible for you to share with me your
gardening story and what you've seen of him as the seasons
come and go. Truly, the whole earth is full of his glory—where I
live, where you live, wherever we are, wherever we garden.

The earth is full of the lovingkindness of the Lord.

—PSALM 33:5, NASB

You say you have not seen him yet in your circumstance? Oh,
then look and listen, and open your heart to hear his voice. God
is still at work in our world, and he is there in your part of it
also. He reaches out in different ways to each of us, but to all of
us he quietly speaks through nature.

Since earliest times men have seen the earth and sky and all God
made, and have known of his existence and great eternal power.

—ROMANS 1:20, TLB

Even the Bible is a book of garden stories. Stories and
parables that plant-lovers of every age can comprehend. Read
about the gourd plant God prepared for Jonah, and the worm
and the wind that helped to teach a lesson. Read about Jesus'
warning through a withered-up fig tree. Read of the wheat field
choked with weeds. Read of the relationship of a vine to its

branches. God's Book is full of gardening stories that challenge the minds of the wisest men.

Who is wise? Let him give heed to these things;
And consider the lovingkindness of the Lord.

—PSALM 107:43, NASB

It is my prayer that as you plant your plot of ground—be it a farm, or a vegetable garden, or herbs in pots sunning on your windowsill, or some ivy in a hanging basket on your balcony— you will sense the presence of God as you go about your work.

Praise him for the growing fields, for they display his greatness.

—PSALM 96:12, TLB

May you see his power as you witness the wonders of seedtime and harvest, season by season.

May you hear his still, small voice in your heart when the storms come and the winds blow.

May each fresh new leaf speak to you of life—and each field lily bring to mind his love.

In His temple everything says, "Glory!"

—PSALM 29:9, NASB

SIXTY-TWO
IN CONCLUSION

This book, you see, is not so much about gardening as about a Gardener—and not so much about earthly projects as about heavenly principles—and not so much about Oklahoma as Eden. My garden has become God's workplace, his schoolroom, and I still have much to learn.

True, I did plant some flowers, and in time they matured. They put down roots, and they put forth blossoms.

What really surprised me is that in the earth-stained, nail-scarred, tender hands of God, I also did some growing. In the Master Gardener's loving care, I, too, am beginning to come into bloom.

He will comfort all her waste places; and he will make her wilderness like Eden, and her desert like the garden of the Lord; joy and gladness shall be found therein, thanksgiving, and the voice of melody.

—ISAIAH 51:3, KJV